HUMMUS

Designed by Eddie Goldfine
Layout by Ariane Rybski
Edited by Shoshana Brickman
Photography by Danya Weiner
"Nutritional Information" by Rachel Granot, B.Sc., M.P.H.

Library of Congress Cataloging-in-Publication Data

Laskin, Avner.
Hummus and 65 other delicious healthy chickpea recipes / Avner Laskin ; photography by Danya Weiner
cm.
ISBN-13: 978-1-4027-3365-9
ISBN-10: 1-4027-3365-8
Cookery (Legumes) 2. Chickpea. I.Title.

TX803.B3L37 2006
641.6'5657—dc22

2006040343

2   4   6   8   10   9   7   5   3   1

Published by Sterling Publishing Co., Inc.
387 Park Avenue South, New York, NY 10016
© 2006 by Penn Publishing Ltd.
Distributed in Canada by Sterling Publishing
c/o Canadian Manda Group, 165 Dufferin Street,
Toronto, Ontario, Canada M6K 3H6
Distributed in the United Kingdom by GMC Distribution Services,
Castle Place, 166 High Street, Lewes, East Sussex, England BN7 1XU
Distributed in Australia by Capricorn Link (Australia) Pty. Ltd.
P.O. Box 704, Windsor, NSW 2756, Australia

Sterling ISBN-13: 978-1-4027-3365-9
ISBN-10: 1-4027-3365-8

For information about custom editions, special sales, premium and
corporate purchases, please contact Sterling Special Sales
Department at 800-805-5489 or specialsales@sterlingpub.com.

AVNER LASKIN
HUMMUS

And 65 Other Delicious & Healthy Chickpea Recipes

PHOTOGRAPHY BY DANYA WEINER

Sterling Publishing Co., Inc.
New York

TABLE OF CONTENTS

ALL ABOUT CHICKPEAS

INTRODUCTION

Chickpeas, also known as garbanzo beans, are a rising star in the realm of nutrition. Everyone seems to have discovered them recently, and to have developed a fancy for their taste, and for the various ways in which they can be served.

These flavorful legumes can be incorporated into a wide variety of foods, ranging from soups and salads to main dishes and savory pastries. Of course, chickpeas also make delicious spreads. In fact, they are probably best known today as the main ingredient in hummus. Falafel is another favorite chickpea-based food. Stuffed into a warm pita and accompanied by fresh salad, falafel makes a tasty snack and satisfying meal-on-the-go.

Combined with chicken or meat, seafood or fish, pasta or rice, chickpeas make an excellent main course. Add to soups and salads to make them heartier and more nourishing. Finely ground into a powder, chickpea flour is used to make breads, pancakes, and fritters.

Chickpeas have been part of the Mediterranean diet for generations. Now they're establishing themselves in North America, and as you'll discover in *Hummus*, the possibilities for preparing them are limitless.

NUTRITIONAL INFORMATION

Chickpeas have remarkable nutritional benefits. They are rich in fiber—the selfsame fiber that is so frequently recommended these days to supplement the Western diet, which has eliminated most of the natural fiber from its food. Nutritional fiber helps in reducing the levels of fat in the blood (cholesterol), retarding the breakdown of the sugars contained in one's food (and, therefore, helping maintain sugar level equilibrium), preventing constipation, and satiating hunger. Fiber is also important in the prevention of intestinal cancer.

Chickpeas include ample quantities of calcium, potassium, magnesium, vitamin C, vitamins of the B group, and even iron! They also contain relatively large amounts of protein. Combining chickpeas with carbohydrates produces a complete protein, making them a perfect meat substitute. No wonder chickpeas are popular with vegetarians—they have all the benefits of beef or chicken, without the fats! This last characteristic of chickpeas, that they contain so little fat, and, therefore, few calories—only 160 calories per 3.5 ounces—makes them a favorite among health enthusiasts and weight-watchers. Since chickpeas have a low glycemic index (that is, they cause sugars to break down slowly in one's blood), they are a great substitute for potatoes, rice, corn, and other carbohydrates. With so many health benefits, chickpeas are simply a wonder food!

In short, there's no end to the benefits of eating chickpeas, so put some in a bowl to soak overnight, stock up on a can or two for your pantry, and get ready to enjoy!

TIPS AND
BASIC RECIPES

Most recipes call for dried chickpeas that are soaked overnight and cooked. In most cases, you can substitute with canned chickpeas if you like, but there is often a difference in the taste and texture. Frozen chickpeas are an excellent substitute for cooked dried chickpeas, although these can be hard to find.

If you are using dried chickpeas, follow the instructions in your recipe. For general guidelines on how to cook dried chickpeas, see page 10.

You may want to cook dried chickpeas in large batches and store them in the freezer until you are ready to use them. Chickpeas can be frozen for up to 2 months. If you are planning to freeze chickpeas, I suggest removing them from the heat a little before they are completely cooked. Finish cooking them when you defrost.

Always defrost and reheat frozen chickpeas before incorporating them into a recipe. Warm chickpeas absorb flavors better than cold chickpeas.

In recipes that require crushed chickpeas, I use a food processor. Some people prefer using a potato masher. It's an excellent alternative, but takes a little more time.

If you have leftover chickpeas that you don't want to freeze, store them in the refrigerator for up to 2 days and simply incorporate them into another meal. Mix chickpeas and sautéed onions to make a savory filling for dough or pastry; combine ground beef, chickpeas, and spices for flavorful meatballs; add chickpeas to pasta sauce for a satisfying and nourishing sauce. The possibilities are endless, delicious, and nutritious.

Several recipes call for chicken soup powder. This can always be substituted by homemade chicken stock; just substitute a cup of chicken stock for each tablespoon of chicken soup powder and cup of water. See page 12 for an excellent chicken stock recipe that can be frozen for up to 4 weeks.

Vegetable stock can be substituted for chicken soup powder in any recipe, just substitute a cup of vegetable stock for each tablespoon of chicken soup powder and cup of water. See page 12 for an easy vegetable stock recipe. You can also substitute 1 tablespoon of vegetable soup powder for each tablespoon of chicken soup powder in any recipe.

All of the hummus recipes (pages 16–31) call for pure tahini, a creamy paste from 100% ground sesame seeds. Pure tahini can be found at many health food shops and Mediterranean food stores.

Several recipes call for chickpea flour, also know as besan or chana flour. Chickpea flour is gluten-free; it can be purchased in health food stores, as well as in many Indian and Italian food shops.

COOKING DRIED CHICKPEAS

The amount of time it takes dried chickpeas to cook depends upon the size and freshness of the chickpeas. Adding baking powder prevents the chickpeas from turning black as they cook, so don't forget to include a teaspoon in every batch of dried chickpeas.

INGREDIENTS

Makes 6 cups

2$\frac{1}{2}$ cups dried chickpeas

20 cups cold water

1 teaspoon baking powder

PREPARATION

1. Soak the chickpeas overnight in 10 cups water.

2. Drain the chickpeas and rinse with cold water.

3. Transfer the chickpeas to a large pot. Add 10 cups water and baking powder, and bring to a boil over high heat.

4. Reduce heat to low and cook uncovered. For chickpeas that are almost soft, cook for about 1$\frac{1}{2}$ hours and drain immediately. For chickpeas that are soft enough to mash in your hands, cook for about 2 hours, let stand for 40 minutes, then drain.

1. Soak the chickpeas overnight in cold water.

2. Drain the chickpeas and rinse with cold water.

CHICKEN STOCK

This stock is rich and flavorful. It can be stored in the refrigerator for up to 3 days, or kept in the freezer for up to 1 month.

INGREDIENTS

Makes 8 cups

3 pounds chicken pieces or bones

2 carrots, peeled and coarsely chopped

2 leeks, coarsely chopped

2 celery stalks, coarsely chopped

2 onions, coarsely chopped

1 tablespoon coarse salt

PREPARATION

1. Put the chicken, carrots, leeks, celery, onion, and salt in a large pot. Cover with water and bring to a boil.

2. Reduce heat and cook for 1½ hours.

3. Strain the stock and discard the solids. Let cool at room temperature.

VEGETABLE STOCK

Feel free to substitute other root vegetables for the ones listed below. This stock can be stored in the refrigerator for up to 3 days or kept in the freezer for up to 2 months.

INGREDIENTS

Makes 8 cups

3 carrots, peeled and coarsely chopped

2 celery stalks, coarsely chopped

1 fennel bulb, coarsely chopped

1 onion, coarsely chopped

2 garlic cloves

1 cup dry white wine

1 teaspoon freshly ground white pepper

1 tablespoon salt

PREPARATION

1. Put the carrots, celery, fennel, onion, garlic, wine, pepper, and salt in a large pot. Cover with water and bring to a boil.

2. Reduce heat and cook for 45 minutes.

3. Strain the stock and discard the solids. Let cool at room temperature.

CROSTINI

Crostini are small toasts made with Italian or French bread, olive oil, and garlic. Topped with creamy butter or sundried tomato paste, they are a delicious accompaniment to hummus, soups, and salads.

INGREDIENTS

Makes 8 slices

8 slices fresh baguette or Italian bread

4 cloves garlic, peeled and halved

2 tablespoons extra virgin olive oil

PREPARATION

1. Heat a grill pan over high heat. Lay the slices of bread flat on the pan and toast until black lines appear. Turn over and repeat on other side.

2. Rub each slice with garlic, drizzle olive oil over top, and serve.

HUMMUS

CREAMY AND SMOOTH HUMMUS

Hummus has a creamy texture that both children and adults love. It makes a great substitute for peanut butter and other sugary spreads.

INGREDIENTS

Serves 12

2½ cups dried chickpeas, soaked overnight in 10 cups cold water

10 cups cold water

1 teaspoon baking powder

4 teaspoons pure tahini

3 tablespoons extra virgin olive oil, plus extra for garnish

½ teaspoon ground cumin

3 tablespoons freshly squeezed lemon juice

Salt

PREPARATION

1. Drain the chickpeas, rinse, and transfer to a large pot. Add the water and baking powder, and bring to a boil over high heat. Reduce heat to low and cook uncovered for 2 hours, or until the chickpeas are soft enough to crush in your hands. Remove from the heat and let stand for 40 minutes.

2. Using a slotted spoon, transfer the chickpeas to the bowl of a food processor fitted with the steel blade. Reserve the cooking liquid for later.

3. Add the tahini, olive oil, cumin, lemon juice, ½ teaspoon salt, and ½ cup of the cooking liquid. Purée into a smooth paste. If the paste is too thick, add a little more cooking liquid. Add salt to taste.

4. Transfer the hummus to a dry container and refrigerate for 3 hours, or until chilled. Serve cold, with a little olive oil drizzled on top.

HUMMUS WITH FRESH HERBS

This dish is light and refreshing—an excellent way to use fresh garden herbs.

INGREDIENTS

Serves 12

2½ cups dried chickpeas, soaked overnight in 10 cups cold water

10 cups cold water

1 teaspoon baking powder

2 cups fresh herbs (parsley, basil, celery, oregano)

4 teaspoons pure tahini

3 tablespoons extra virgin olive oil, plus extra for garnish

½ teaspoon ground cumin

3 tablespoons freshly squeezed lemon juice

Salt

PREPARATION

1. Drain the chickpeas, rinse, and transfer to a large pot. Add the water and baking powder, and bring to a boil over high heat. Reduce heat to low and cook uncovered for 2 hours, or until the chickpeas are soft enough to crush in your hands. Remove from the heat and let stand for 40 minutes.

2. In the meantime, place the fresh herbs in the bowl of your food processor and purée with the steel blade into a smooth paste.

3. Using a slotted spoon, transfer the chickpeas to the bowl of the food processor. Reserve the cooking liquid for later.

4. Add the tahini, olive oil, cumin, lemon juice, ½ teaspoon salt, and ½ cup of the cooking liquid. Purée into a smooth paste. If the paste is too thick, add a little more cooking liquid. Add salt to taste.

5. Transfer to a dry container and refrigerate for 3 hours, or until the hummus is chilled. Serve cold, with a little olive oil drizzled on top.

HUMMUS WITH COARSELY GROUND CHICKPEAS

This hummus is a little chunkier than the traditional version. It makes a great dip for fresh vegetables or oven-baked nachos.

INGREDIENTS

Serves 12

2$\frac{1}{2}$ cups dried chickpeas, soaked overnight in 10 cups cold water

10 cups cold water

1 teaspoon baking powder

4 teaspoons pure tahini

3 tablespoons extra virgin olive oil, plus extra for garnish

$\frac{1}{2}$ teaspoon ground cumin

3 tablespoons freshly squeezed lemon juice

Salt

PREPARATION

1. Drain the chickpeas, rinse, and transfer to a large pot. Add the water and baking powder, and bring to a boil over high heat. Reduce heat to low and cook uncovered for 2 hours, or until the chickpeas are soft enough to crush in your hands. Remove from the heat and let stand for 40 minutes.

2. Using a slotted spoon, transfer $\frac{2}{3}$ of the chickpeas to the bowl of a food processor fitted with the steel blade. Reserve the cooking liquid for later.

3. Add the tahini, olive oil, cumin, lemon juice, $\frac{1}{2}$ teaspoon salt, and $\frac{1}{2}$ cup of the cooking liquid. Purée into a smooth paste. If the paste is too thick, add a little more cooking liquid.

4. Separately, coarsely crush the remaining $\frac{1}{3}$ of the chickpeas with a fork. Use a wooden spoon to stir the crushed chickpeas into the chickpea paste. Add salt to taste.

5. Transfer the hummus to a dry container and refrigerate for 3 hours, or until chilled. Serve cold, with a little olive oil drizzled on top.

SPICY HUMMUS

*This dish is perfect for people who like their food piquant. If you're having
company, you may want to serve it with a bowl of Hummus with
Fresh Herbs (page 17), for guests who prefer a milder flavor.*

INGREDIENTS

Serves 12

2½ cups dried chickpeas,
soaked overnight in 10 cups
cold water

10 cups cold water

1 teaspoon baking powder

4 teaspoons pure tahini

3 tablespoons extra virgin
olive oil

1 tablespoon Mexican chili
sauce

½ teaspoon finely ground hot
red pepper flakes

3 tablespoons freshly squeezed
lemon juice

Salt

Chili oil, for garnish

PREPARATION

1. Drain the chickpeas, rinse, and
transfer to a large pot. Add the
water and baking powder, and
bring to a boil over high heat.
Reduce heat to low and cook
uncovered for 2 hours, or until
the chickpeas are soft enough to
crush in your hands. Remove
from the heat and let stand for
40 minutes.

2. Using a slotted spoon, transfer
the chickpeas to the bowl of a
food processor fitted with the
steel blade. Reserve the cooking
liquid for later.

3. Add the tahini, olive oil, chili
sauce, red pepper flakes, lemon
juice, ½ teaspoon salt, and ½ cup
of the cooking liquid. Purée into
a smooth paste. If the paste is too
thick, add a little more cooking
liquid. Add salt to taste.

4. Transfer the hummus to a
dry container and refrigerate for
3 hours, or until chilled. Drizzle
some chili oil over top and serve
cold, with a side of tortilla chips.

MASBACHA

The use of whole chickpeas in this hummus gives it a slightly different texture;
the addition of hot green peppers makes it a little spicy. Unlike most types of
hummus, this dish is best served warm.

INGREDIENTS

Serves 12

2½ cups dried chickpeas, soaked overnight in 10 cups cold water

10 cups cold water, plus 2 tablespoons

1 teaspoon baking powder

3 cloves garlic, peeled

4 teaspoons pure tahini

12 tablespoons freshly squeezed lemon juice

Salt

1 tablespoon extra virgin olive oil, plus extra for garnish

½ hot green pepper, cut in half and seeded

1 clove garlic, crushed

PREPARATION

1. Drain the chickpeas, rinse, and transfer to a large pot. Add the water, baking powder, and garlic, and bring to a boil over high heat. Reduce heat to low and cook uncovered for 1½ hours, or until the chickpeas are soft. Drain and reserve the cooking liquid for later use.

2. Set aside 5 tablespoons of whole chickpeas and transfer the rest to the bowl of a food processor fitted with the steel blade. Process until smooth and uniform.

3. While the processor is operating, gradually add the tahini, 6 tablespoons lemon juice, and ½ teaspoon salt. Slowly add ½ cup of the cooking liquid until the texture resembles thick porridge. Add more cooking liquid as necessary.

4. Add the olive oil, then turn off the machine. Set aside, but do not refrigerate, as this dish is served warm.

5. To make the sauce, put the remaining 2 tablespoons water, 6 tablespoons lemon juice, hot pepper, garlic, and salt to taste in a blender. Blend until uniform. Pour through a strainer into a clean bowl.

6. Spread a generous layer of warm hummus in the middle of a plate. Top with a tablespoon of whole chickpeas and 2 tablespoons of sauce. Drizzle olive oil over top and serve.

HUMMUS WITH GROUND MEAT AND PINE NUTS

The addition of pine nuts gives this hummus recipe a buttery flavor and distinct crunchy texture.

INGREDIENTS

Serves 12

2½ cups dried chickpeas, soaked overnight in 10 cups cold water

10 cups cold water

1 teaspoon baking powder

4 teaspoons pure tahini

5 tablespoons extra virgin olive oil

3 tablespoons freshly squeezed lemon juice

½ teaspoon ground cumin

Salt and freshly ground black pepper

1 onion, finely chopped

1 pound freshly ground beef or lamb

2 cloves garlic, minced

½ cup pine nuts

1 tablespoon ground sumac

¼ cup chopped fresh parsley, plus extra for garnish

PREPARATION

1. Drain the chickpeas, rinse, and transfer to a large pot. Add the water and baking powder, and bring to a boil over high heat. Reduce heat to low and cook uncovered for 2 hours, or until the chickpeas are soft enough to crush in your hands. Remove from the heat and let stand for 40 minutes.

2. Using a slotted spoon, transfer the chickpeas to the bowl of a food processor fitted with the steel blade. Reserve the cooking liquid for later.

3. Add the tahini, 3 tablespoons olive oil, lemon juice, cumin, ½ teaspoon salt, and ½ cup of the cooking liquid. Purée into a smooth paste. If the paste is too thick, add a little more cooking liquid. Add salt to taste.

4. Transfer the hummus to a dry container and refrigerate for 3 hours, or until chilled.

5. About 30 minutes before serving, heat the remaining 2 tablespoons olive oil in a large skillet over medium heat. Add the onion and sauté until golden.

6. Add the beef and garlic and sauté for 20 minutes.

7. Stir in the pine nuts and sumac, and add salt and pepper to taste. Sauté for 5 more minutes.

8. Remove from the heat, add the parsley, and mix well.

9. To serve, spread the hummus generously on a large plate. Top with the meat mixture and garnish with parsley.

HUMMUS WITH FAVA BEANS

Fava beans, known as **foule** *in the Middle East, are a common accompaniment to chickpea dishes and hummus. Served with fresh pita, this dish is particularly hearty and satisfying.*

INGREDIENTS

Serves 12

2½ cups dried chickpeas, soaked overnight in 10 cups cold water

14 cups cold water

1 teaspoon baking powder

1 cup dried fava beans, soaked overnight in 4 cups cold water

1 teaspoon ground cumin

Salt and freshly ground black pepper

4 teaspoons pure tahini

3 tablespoons extra virgin olive oil, plus extra for garnish

3 tablespoons freshly squeezed lemon juice

PREPARATION

1. Drain the chickpeas, rinse, and transfer to a large pot. Add 10 cups water and baking powder, and bring to a boil over high heat.

2. Separately, drain the fava beans and transfer to a medium pot. Add the remaining 4 cups water, cumin, 1 teaspoon salt, and ½ teaspoon pepper, and bring to a boil over high heat.

3. Reduce the heat on both pots and cook uncovered for 2 hours, or until the beans are soft enough to crush in your hands.

4. Set the chickpeas aside for 40 minutes. Set the fava beans aside.

5. Using a slotted spoon, transfer the chickpeas to the bowl of a food processor fitted with the steel blade. Reserve the cooking liquid for later.

6. Add the tahini, olive oil, lemon juice, ½ teaspoon salt, and ½ cup of the cooking liquid. Purée into a smooth paste. If the paste is too thick, add a little more cooking liquid. Add salt to taste.

7. Transfer the hummus to a dry container and refrigerate for 3 hours, or until chilled.

8. Reheat the fava beans just before serving. Spread a layer of hummus on a plate, top with 1 or 2 tablespoons of warm fava beans, and drizzle a little olive oil over top.

ROASTED GARLIC HUMMUS

Garlic is believed to have countless health benefits, from reducing blood pressure to fighting off the common cold. Garlic also tastes great, especially when roasted, which makes this garlic-rich hummus a perfect dish to satisfy all your senses.

INGREDIENTS

Serves 12

2½ cups dried chickpeas, soaked overnight in 10 cups cold water

10 cups cold water

1 teaspoon baking powder

4 teaspoons pure tahini

½ cup plus 3 tablespoons extra virgin olive oil

½ teaspoon ground cumin

3 tablespoons freshly squeezed lemon juice

Salt and freshly ground black pepper

15 cloves garlic, peeled

PREPARATION

1. Drain the chickpeas, rinse, and transfer to a large pot. Add the water and baking powder, and bring to a boil over high heat. Reduce heat to low and cook uncovered for 2 hours, or until the chickpeas are soft enough to crush in your hands. Remove from the heat and let stand for 40 minutes.

2. Using a slotted spoon, transfer the chickpeas to the bowl of a food processor fitted with the steel blade. Reserve the cooking liquid for later.

3. Add the tahini, 3 tablespoons of olive oil, cumin, lemon juice, ½ teaspoon salt, and ½ cup of the cooking liquid. Purée into a smooth paste. If the paste is too thick, add a little more cooking liquid. Add salt to taste.

4. In a small pot, place the garlic and remaining ½ cup olive oil. Cook covered over low heat for 30 minutes, or until soft.

5. Transfer the garlic to a small bowl and crush with a fork until the texture is a coarse paste. Add salt and pepper to taste.

6. Spread a generous layer of hummus on a plate and top with roasted garlic. Serve with fresh bread, focaccia, or pita.

HUMMUS WITH SAUTÉED MUSHROOMS

Your kitchen will be filled with the aromatic scent of sautéing mushrooms as you prepare the topping for this hummus.

INGREDIENTS

Serves 12

2½ cups dried chickpeas, soaked overnight in 10 cups cold water

10 cups cold water

1 teaspoon baking powder

4 teaspoons pure tahini

5 tablespoons extra virgin olive oil, plus extra for garnish

3 tablespoons freshly squeezed lemon juice

Salt and freshly ground black pepper

1 onion, finely chopped

2 cloves garlic, minced

½ pound champignon mushrooms, halved lengthwise

PREPARATION

1. Drain the chickpeas, rinse, and transfer to a large pot. Add the water and baking powder, and bring to a boil over high heat. Reduce heat to low and cook uncovered for 2 hours, or until the chickpeas are soft enough to crush in your hands. Remove from the heat and let stand for 40 minutes.

2. Using a slotted spoon, transfer the chickpeas to the bowl of a food processor fitted with the steel blade. Reserve the cooking liquid for later.

3. Add the tahini, 3 tablespoons of olive oil, lemon juice, ½ teaspoon salt, and ½ cup of the cooking liquid. Purée into a smooth paste. If the paste is too thick, add a little more cooking liquid. Add salt to taste.

4. Transfer the hummus to a dry container and refrigerate for 3 hours, or until chilled.

5. About 15 minutes before serving, heat the remaining 2 tablespoons olive oil over medium heat in a large skillet. Add the onion and sauté until golden.

6. Add the garlic and mushrooms and sauté while stirring for 10 minutes. Add salt and pepper to taste and sauté for 2 minutes.

7. To serve, spread a thick layer of hummus on a plate or fresh bread, and top with a generous spoonful of sautéed mushrooms.

HUMMUS WITH SAUTÉED ONIONS

Serve this hummus on a soft tortilla for a vegetarian version of the classic beef fajita.

INGREDIENTS

Serves 12

2½ cups dried chickpeas, soaked overnight in 10 cups cold water

10 cups cold water

1 teaspoon baking powder

4 teaspoons pure tahini

6 tablespoons extra virgin olive oil, plus extra for garnish

½ teaspoon ground cumin

3 tablespoons freshly squeezed lemon juice

Salt and freshly ground black pepper

3 large onions, thinly sliced

1 ripe tomato, finely chopped

2 tablespoons chopped fresh parsley, for garnish

PREPARATION

1. Drain the chickpeas, rinse, and transfer to a large pot. Add the water and baking powder, and bring to a boil over high heat. Reduce heat to low and cook uncovered for 2 hours, or until the chickpeas are soft enough to crush in your hands. Remove from the heat and let stand for 40 minutes.

2. Using a slotted spoon, transfer the chickpeas to the bowl of a food processor fitted with the steel blade. Reserve the cooking liquid for later.

3. Add the tahini, 3 tablespoons olive oil, cumin, lemon juice, ½ teaspoon salt, and ½ cup of the cooking liquid. Purée into a smooth paste. If the paste is too thick, add a little more cooking liquid. Add salt to taste. Transfer the hummus to a dry container and refrigerate for 3 hours, or until chilled.

4. About 10 minutes before serving, heat the remaining 3 tablespoons olive oil in a skillet over medium heat. Add the onion and sauté until golden. Remove from the heat and mix in the tomato. Add salt and pepper to taste.

5. Spread the hummus on a warm tortilla or serving dish. Top with sautéed onions and garnish with olive oil and parsley.

SALADS

ROASTED FENNEL WITH CHICKPEAS

The combination of colors in this recipe makes it a feast for the eyes as well as the palate.

INGREDIENTS

Serves 6

2 cups dried chickpeas, soaked overnight in 8 cups cold water

8 cups cold water

1 teaspoon baking powder

4 medium fennel bulbs

1 cup white wine

¼ cup extra virgin olive oil

2 cloves garlic, crushed

Salt and freshly ground white pepper

2 oranges, peeled

3 tablespoons freshly squeezed lemon juice

PREPARATION

1. Drain the chickpeas, rinse, and transfer to a large pot. Add the water and baking powder, and bring to a boil over high heat. Reduce heat to low and cook uncovered for 1½ hours, or until the chickpeas are soft. Drain and place in a large bowl.

2. Preheat the oven to 300°F.

3. Slice the fennel lengthwise into thin strips and lay in a deep pan.

4. Add the wine, olive oil, garlic, 1 teaspoon salt, and ½ teaspoon pepper, and mix well with a wooden spoon.

5. Spread the mixture evenly in the pan and bake for 45 minutes, or until the fennel is soft and has absorbed most of the liquid.

6. In the meantime, separate the oranges into sections, and carefully remove the membrane from each section using a paring knife.

7. Transfer the roasted fennel to the bowl with the chickpeas and mix well. Add orange sections, lemon juice, and salt and pepper to taste. Transfer to a serving dish and serve.

CALAMARI AND CHICKPEA SALAD

*Calamari and chickpeas are staple ingredients in the Mediterranean diet.
With the addition of red cherry tomatoes and bright green arugula, this salad
becomes a celebration of colors and textures.*

INGREDIENTS

Serves 4

2 cups dried chickpeas, soaked overnight in 8 cups cold water

8 cups cold water

1 teaspoon baking powder

3 tablespoons extra virgin olive oil, plus more for garnish

½ pound calamari, bodies and tentacles, cut into ½-inch pieces

Salt and freshly ground white pepper

2 fresh red chili peppers, seeded, halved lengthwise, and cut into thin strips

15 cherry tomatoes, quartered

3 tablespoons fresh lemon juice

2 cloves garlic, minced

1 bunch arugula

PREPARATION

1. Drain the chickpeas, rinse, and transfer to a large pot. Add the water and baking powder, and bring to a boil over high heat. Reduce heat to low and cook uncovered for 1½ hours, or until the chickpeas are soft. Drain, remove the peels of the chickpeas, and set aside.

2. In a heavy skillet, heat 1 tablespoon of olive oil over high heat. Add the calamari and sauté for 3 or 4 minutes, until the calamari is white. Add salt and pepper, remove from heat, and set aside.

3. Combine the chickpeas, calamari, chili peppers, and tomatoes in a large bowl. Add the remaining 2 tablespoons olive oil, lemon juice, garlic, and salt and pepper to taste. Mix well and set aside for 30 minutes for the flavors to absorb.

4. Mix the arugula into the salad just before serving. Transfer to a serving dish and drizzle olive oil over top.

GREEN BEAN AND CHICKPEA SALAD

Use fresh green beans straight from your garden for a salad that is bursting with summer flavors.

INGREDIENTS

Serves 6

2 cups dried chickpeas, soaked overnight in 8 cups cold water

12 cups cold water

1 teaspoon baking powder

1 tablespoon coarse salt

$\frac{1}{2}$ pound fresh green beans, trimmed

3 tablespoons extra virgin olive oil

1 tablespoon red wine vinegar

1 clove garlic, crushed

1 teaspoon salt

$\frac{1}{2}$ teaspoon freshly ground white pepper

1 tablespoon chopped fresh parsley

PREPARATION

1. Drain the chickpeas, rinse, and transfer to a large pot. Add 10 cups water and baking powder, and bring to a boil over high heat. Reduce heat to low and cook uncovered for $1\frac{1}{2}$ hours, or until the chickpeas are soft. Drain and transfer to a large bowl.

2. Place the remaining 4 cups water and coarse salt in a pot and bring to a boil.

3. Add the green beans and cook for 4 minutes.

4. Drain the beans and transfer to the bowl with the chickpeas. Add olive oil, vinegar, garlic, salt, pepper, and parsley. Mix well and transfer to a serving dish.

ROASTED PEPPERS WITH CHICKPEAS

Roasted peppers taste excellent after the flavors have had a chance to set. If possible, prepare the peppers a day in advance; combine them with the chickpeas and arugula just before serving.

INGREDIENTS

Serves 6

6 medium red peppers

Salt and freshly ground white pepper

3 tablespoons extra virgin olive oil

1 tablespoon red wine vinegar

2 cloves garlic, minced

1 tablespoon chopped fresh thyme leaves

2 cups dried chickpeas, soaked overnight in 8 cups cold water

8 cups cold water

1 teaspoon baking powder

Handful fresh arugula

PREPARATION

1. Preheat the oven to 400°F.

2. Place the peppers on a baking sheet and roast for 30 minutes, or until the skin is charred.

3. Immediately transfer the peppers to a bowl and cover with plastic wrap so that the peppers are completely sealed. Set aside for 15 minutes, or until the peppers are cool enough to touch.

4. Remove the plastic wrap, hold the peppers over the bowl, and peel off the skin. Discard the skins and transfer the peppers to a clean bowl. Do not rinse the peppers, as this damages their flavor. Pour any liquid from the first bowl through a strainer and into the bowl with the peppers.

5. Add 1 teaspoon salt, ½ teaspoon pepper, olive oil, vinegar, garlic, and thyme to the peppers, and mix well. Refrigerate until ready to serve.

6. Drain the chickpeas, rinse, and transfer to a large pot. Add the water and baking powder, and bring to a boil over high heat. Reduce heat to low and cook uncovered for 1½ hours, or until the chickpeas are soft. Drain and transfer to a large bowl.

7. Just before serving, mix the roasted peppers and arugula with the chickpeas. Add salt and pepper to taste and transfer to a serving dish.

TOMATO, SPINACH, AND CHICKPEA SALAD

Bright and colorful, this salad is a Mediterranean alternative to the traditional spinach salad.

INGREDIENTS

Serves 6

2 cups dried chickpeas, soaked overnight in 8 cups cold water

8 cups cold water

1 teaspoon baking powder

15 cherry tomatoes, quartered

1/2 pound fresh spinach leaves

3 tablespoons extra virgin olive oil

2 tablespoons freshly squeezed lemon juice

1 tablespoon balsamic vinegar

3 tablespoons grated Parmesan cheese

1 tablespoon salt

1/2 teaspoon freshly ground black pepper

PREPARATION

1. Drain the chickpeas, rinse, and transfer to a large pot. Add the water and baking powder, and bring to a boil over high heat. Reduce heat to low and cook uncovered for 1$\frac{1}{2}$ hours, or until the chickpeas are soft. Drain and transfer to a large bowl.

2. Add the tomatoes and spinach and mix gently.

3. Add the olive oil, lemon juice, balsamic vinegar, Parmesan, salt, and pepper. Mix well and transfer to a serving dish.

CHICKPEA AND ARTICHOKE SALAD

Marinated artichokes have a tangy taste and silky texture. They are an excellent complement to the nutty flavor and subtle crunch of freshly cooked chickpeas.

INGREDIENTS

Serves 6

2 cups dried chickpeas, soaked overnight in 8 cups cold water

8 cups cold water

1 teaspoon baking powder

15 cherry tomatoes, quartered

10 marinated artichoke hearts, quartered

3 tablespoons extra virgin olive oil, plus more for garnish

3 tablespoons fresh lemon juice

1 garlic clove, minced

1 teaspoon salt

$\frac{1}{2}$ teaspoon freshly ground white pepper

1 tablespoon chopped fresh parsley

1 tablespoon coarsely chopped fresh basil leaves

PREPARATION

1. Drain the chickpeas, rinse, and transfer to a large pot. Add the water and baking powder, and bring to a boil over high heat. Reduce heat to low and cook uncovered for $1\frac{1}{2}$ hours, or until the chickpeas are soft. Drain and transfer to a large bowl.

2. Add the tomatoes and artichoke hearts and mix gently.

3. Mix in the olive oil, lemon juice, garlic, salt, and pepper. Refrigerate for 30 minutes.

4. Add the parsley and basil, and mix well. Transfer to a serving dish and serve.

THAI CHICKPEA SALAD

*This salad calls for Thai fish sauce, known as **nam bplah** in Thai. It is an aromatic, salty, and distinct sauce that can be found in many large supermarkets and Asian food stores.*

INGREDIENTS

Serves 6

2 cups dried chickpeas, soaked overnight in 8 cups cold water

8 cups cold water

1 teaspoon baking powder

1 firm mango, peeled and cut lengthwise into thin strips

1 tablespoon Thai fish sauce

1 teaspoon sweet chili sauce

1 teaspoon sesame oil

$\frac{1}{2}$ teaspoon salt

$\frac{1}{2}$ teaspoon freshly ground white pepper

4 tablespoons freshly squeezed lime juice

1 tablespoon chopped fresh coriander

1 tablespoon coarsely chopped fresh basil leaves

PREPARATION

1. Drain the chickpeas, rinse, and transfer to a large pot. Add the water and baking powder, and bring to a boil over high heat. Reduce heat to low and cook uncovered for $1\frac{1}{2}$ hours, or until the chickpeas are soft. Drain and transfer to a large bowl.

2. Add the mango, fish sauce, chili sauce, sesame oil, salt, pepper, and lime juice, and mix well. Refrigerate for 1 hour.

3. Remove from the refrigerator, add the coriander and basil, and mix well. Transfer to a serving dish and serve.

WARM SHRIMP AND CHICKPEA SALAD

The flavors in this dish blend best when warm, so be sure to reheat the chickpeas if necessary before mixing in the sautéed shrimp.

INGREDIENTS

Serves 6

2 cups dried chickpeas, soaked overnight in 8 cups cold water

8 cups cold water

1 teaspoon baking powder

1 green chili pepper, seeded and coarsely chopped

3 tablespoons fresh lemon juice

2 tablespoons chopped fresh parsley

3 tablespoons extra virgin olive oil

3 cloves garlic, minced

Salt and freshly ground black pepper

10 large shrimp

2 large ripe tomatoes, cut into wedges

PREPARATION

1. Drain the chickpeas, rinse, and transfer to a large pot. Add the water and baking powder, and bring to a boil over high heat. Reduce heat to low and cook uncovered for 1½ hours, or until the chickpeas are soft. Drain and transfer to a large bowl.

2. In the meantime, place the chili pepper, lemon juice, parsley, 1 tablespoon of olive oil, 1 clove of garlic, and a pinch of salt in a blender or food processor and blend until smooth.

3. Heat the remaining 2 tablespoons olive oil in a heavy skillet over high heat. Add the remaining 2 cloves of garlic and sauté until golden.

4. Add the shrimp, 1 teaspoon salt, and ½ teaspoon pepper and sauté until the shrimp is charred on both sides.

5. If the chickpeas have cooled, put them in a pot with boiling water for 2 minutes to warm and drain. Add the chili sauce and shrimp to the warm chickpeas. Pour in any remaining juices in the skillet as well. Mix in the tomatoes and add salt and pepper to taste. Transfer to a serving dish and serve immediately.

CHICKPEA AND CITRUS SALAD

Juicy oranges and sweet clementines make this salad light and refreshing, perfect for a Sunday brunch.

INGREDIENTS

Serves 6

2 cups dried chickpeas, soaked overnight in 8 cups cold water

8 cups cold water

1 teaspoon baking powder

2 oranges, peeled

1 clementine, peeled

2 tablespoons extra virgin olive oil

1 teaspoon salt

$\frac{1}{2}$ teaspoon freshly ground white pepper

2 cups baby salad greens

2 tablespoons freshly squeezed lemon juice

PREPARATION

1. Drain the chickpeas, rinse, and transfer to a large pot. Add the water and baking powder, and bring to a boil over high heat. Reduce heat to low and cook uncovered for $1\frac{1}{2}$ hours, or until the chickpeas are soft. Drain and transfer to a large bowl.

2. Separate the oranges and clementine into sections and carefully remove the membrane from each section using a paring knife. Place in a bowl with olive oil, salt, and pepper, and mix well. Refrigerate for 30 minutes.

3. Toss in the salad greens just before serving. Add the lemon juice, mix well, and transfer to a serving dish.

SARDINE, AVOCADO, AND CHICKPEA SALAD

This salad is rich in protein, iron, and calcium. If possible, prepare the roasted peppers a day in advance so the flavors have a chance to blend overnight.

INGREDIENTS

Serves 6

3 medium red peppers

3 tablespoons extra virgin olive oil

1/2 tablespoon red wine vinegar

1 clove garlic, minced

1/2 tablespoon chopped fresh thyme leaves

Salt and freshly ground white pepper

2 cups dried chickpeas, soaked overnight in 8 cups cold water

8 cups cold water

1 teaspoon baking powder

1/2 pound fresh sardines, cleaned and with heads removed

3 tablespoons freshly squeezed lemon juice

1 head romaine lettuce

1 ripe avocado, peeled and cut into 1/4-inch slices

1 bunch arugula

PREPARATION

1. Preheat the oven to 400°F.

2. Place the peppers on a baking sheet and roast for 30 minutes, or until the skin is charred.

3. Immediately transfer the peppers to a bowl and cover with plastic wrap so that the peppers are completely sealed. Set aside for about 15 minutes, or until the peppers are cool enough to touch.

4. Remove the plastic wrap, hold the peppers over the bowl, and peel off the skin. Discard the skins and transfer the peppers to a clean bowl. Do not rinse the peppers, as this damages their flavor. Pour any liquid from the first bowl through a strainer and into the bowl with the peppers.

5. Add 2 tablespoons olive oil, vinegar, garlic, thyme, 1/2 tea-spoon salt, and 1/2 teaspoon pepper and mix well. Refrigerate until ready to serve. If possible, refrigerate overnight as this gives the flavors a chance to be absorbed.

6. Drain the chickpeas, rinse, and transfer to a large pot. Add the water and baking powder, and bring to a boil over high heat. Reduce heat to low and cook uncovered for 1 1/2 hours, or until the chickpeas are soft. Drain and transfer to a large bowl.

7. Arrange the sardines skin-side down on a large plate. Sprinkle 1 teaspoon salt over top. Drizzle lemon juice and remaining tablespoon olive oil and refrigerate for 30 minutes.

8. Remove from the refrigerator and transfer the sardines, along with the juices on the plate, to the bowl with the chickpeas.

9. Add the lettuce, roasted peppers, avocado, and arugula. Add salt and pepper to taste, mix gently, and transfer to a serving dish.

BULGUR, CHICKEN, AND CHICKPEA SALAD

Bulgur wheat is a staple grain in the Mediterranean diet. Light tasting and remarkably easy to prepare, it's a natural companion for chickpeas.

INGREDIENTS

Serves 6

1½ cups bulgur wheat

14 cups cold water

1 cup dried chickpeas, soaked overnight in 4 cups cold water

1 teaspoon baking powder

2 tablespoons chopped fresh parsley

2 tablespoons extra virgin olive oil

3 tablespoons freshly squeezed lemon juice

Salt and freshly ground black pepper

½ pound boneless, skinless chicken breasts, cut into ½-inch chunks

1 clove garlic, minced

PREPARATION

1. Place the bulgur in 10 cups water and let stand for 3 hours.

2. In the meantime, drain the chickpeas, rinse, and transfer to a large pot. Add remaining 4 cups water and baking powder, and bring to a boil over high heat. Reduce heat to low and cook uncovered for 1½ hours, or until the chickpeas are soft. Drain and transfer to a large bowl.

3. Drain the bulgur well, pressing out all of the water, and transfer to the bowl with the chickpeas.

4. Add the parsley, 1 tablespoon of olive oil, lemon juice, ½ teaspoon salt, and ¼ teaspoon pepper. Mix well and set aside.

5. Heat the remaining tablespoon olive oil in a heavy skillet over high heat. Add the chicken, garlic, ½ teaspoon salt, and ½ teaspoon pepper, and sauté until golden.

6. Add the chicken to the chickpeas and bulgur and mix well. Add salt and pepper to taste, transfer to a serving dish, and serve warm.

CHICKPEAS WITH SPINACH AND LEMON

The heart-like shape and warm color of the chickpeas is particulary noticeable in this salad thanks to the contrast with the soft green spinach.

INGREDIENTS

Serves 6

2 cups dried chickpeas, soaked overnight in 8 cups cold water

8 cups cold water

1 teaspoon baking powder

2 pounds fresh spinach leaves

Salt and freshly ground black pepper

$\frac{1}{2}$ cup extra virgin olive oil

3 tablespoons freshly squeezed lemon juice

PREPARATION

1. Drain the chickpeas, rinse, and transfer to a large pot. Add the water and baking powder, and bring to a boil over high heat. Reduce heat to low and cook uncovered for $1\frac{1}{2}$ hours, or until the chickpeas are almost soft. Drain and transfer to a large bowl.

2. Place the spinach and 1 teaspoon salt in a large pot and cook covered over low heat for 5 minutes. Transfer to a colander and drain.

3. Heat the olive oil in a large pan over low heat. Mix in the chickpeas and lemon juice and cook for 3 minutes.

4. Add the spinach, 1 teaspoon salt, and 1 teaspoon pepper, and cook over medium heat for 15 minutes, stirring occasionally.

5. Transfer to individual serving dishes and serve immediately.

SOUPS

TOMATO AND CHICKPEA SOUP

Traditional tomato soup gains a Mediterranean touch thanks to the addition of chickpeas in this recipe. Serve with salted crackers or crispy breadsticks.

INGREDIENTS

Serves 8

2 cups dried chickpeas, soaked overnight in 8 cups cold water

2 tablespoons extra virgin olive oil, plus extra for garnish

1 onion, chopped

2 cloves garlic, minced

2 celery stalks, chopped

Salt and freshly ground black pepper

1 16-ounce can plum tomatoes, peeled and diced

2½ cups cold water

2 tablespoons chicken soup powder

10 fresh basil leaves, chopped

2 tablespoons grated Parmesan cheese, for garnish

PREPARATION

1. Transfer the chickpeas to a colander and rinse with cold water.

2. In a large soup pot, heat the olive oil over low heat. Add the onion, garlic, celery, and ½ teaspoon salt, and cook until soft.

3. Add the chickpeas, tomatoes, and water, and bring to a boil over high heat.

4. Reduce heat and add soup powder, salt, and pepper. Cover and simmer for 2 hours.

5. Add the basil just before serving and mix well. Transfer to serving bowls and garnish with olive oil, pepper, and Parmesan.

MUSHROOM AND CHICKPEA SOUP

Use a combination of fresh champignon and cremini mushrooms to make a soup with a rich flavor and inviting aroma.

INGREDIENTS

Serves 8

2 cups dried chickpeas, soaked overnight in 8 cups cold water

2 tablespoons extra virgin olive oil

1 onion, chopped

2 cloves garlic, minced

1 tablespoon chopped fresh thyme leaves

1 celery stalk, finely chopped

½ teaspoon freshly ground nutmeg

Salt and freshly ground white pepper

1 pound fresh mixed mushrooms, sliced

½ cup white wine

2½ cups cold water

2 tablespoons chicken soup powder

½ pound heavy cream

PREPARATION

1. Transfer the chickpeas to a colander and rinse with cold water.

2. In a large soup pot, heat the olive oil over low heat. Add the onion, garlic, thyme, celery, nutmeg, and ½ teaspoon salt, and cook until soft.

3. Add the mushrooms and continue cooking until the mushrooms are soft and aromatic.

4. Pour in the wine, increase the heat, and cook for 5 minutes, or until the liquid evaporates.

5. Add the chickpeas and water, and bring to a boil.

6. Reduce heat, add soup powder, salt, and pepper. Cover and simmer for 2 hours.

7. Pour in the cream and cook for 10 minutes over low heat. Transfer to serving bowls and serve.

ITALIAN CHICKPEA SOUP

This soup makes a comforting and satisfying meal. Served with fresh bread or crisp crostini (page 13), it makes an excellent lunch or afternoon snack.

INGREDIENTS

Serves 8

2 cups dried chickpeas, soaked overnight in 8 cups cold water

2 tablespoons extra virgin olive oil, plus extra for garnish

1 onion, chopped

1 clove garlic, minced

Salt and freshly ground black pepper

2 large potatoes, peeled and cut into $\frac{1}{2}$-inch dice

3 cups cold water

1 cup tomato juice

2 tablespoons chicken soup powder

$\frac{1}{4}$ pound shell pasta

10 fresh basil leaves, chopped

PREPARATION

1. Transfer the chickpeas to a colander and rinse with cold water.

2. In a large soup pot, heat the olive oil over low heat. Add the onion, garlic, and $\frac{1}{2}$ teaspoon salt and cook until soft.

3. Add the chickpeas, potatoes, water, and tomato juice, and bring to a boil over high heat.

4. Reduce heat and add soup powder, salt, and pepper. Cover and simmer for 2 hours.

5. Add the pasta and basil and cook uncovered for 30 minutes.

6. Transfer to serving bowls and garnish with olive oil and black pepper.

GREEN SOUP WITH CHICKPEAS

With chard and spinach, this colorful soup is brimming with vitamins and minerals.

INGREDIENTS

Serves 8

2 cups dried chickpeas, soaked overnight in 8 cups cold water

2 tablespoons extra virgin olive oil

1 onion, chopped

2 cloves garlic, minced

2 celery stalks, chopped

Salt and freshly ground black pepper

$\frac{1}{2}$ pound chard, finely chopped

$\frac{1}{2}$ pound spinach leaves, finely chopped

2 large potatoes, peeled and cut into $\frac{1}{2}$-inch dice

$2\frac{1}{2}$ cups cold water

2 tablespoons chicken soup powder

6 $\frac{1}{2}$-inch dice of butter, for garnish

PREPARATION

1. Transfer the chickpeas to a colander and rinse with cold water.

2. In a large soup pot, heat the olive oil over low heat. Add the onion, garlic, celery, and $\frac{1}{2}$ teaspoon salt, and cook until soft.

3. Mix in the chard and cook for 15 minutes, or until soft.

4. Add the chickpeas, spinach, potatoes, and water, and bring to a boil over high heat.

5. Reduce heat and add soup powder, salt, and pepper. Cover and simmer for 2 hours.

6. Transfer to serving bowls and garnish with a cube of butter.

HARARE SOUP

With lentils, beef, and spaghetti, this soup is hearty and heartwarming—a perfect meal on a chilly winter evening.

INGREDIENTS

Serves 8

1 cup dried chickpeas, soaked overnight in 5 cups cold water

2 tablespoons extra virgin olive oil, plus extra for garnish

2 onions, finely chopped

5 cloves garlic, minced

5 celery stalks, chopped

Salt and freshly ground black pepper

2 pounds lean beef, cut into 1-inch dice

3 marrow bones

1 cup lentils, picked over and rinsed

1 16-ounce can plum tomatoes, peeled and crushed

$1/4$ cup tomato paste

5 cups cold water

$1/2$ cup all-purpose flour

$1/2$ cups chopped fresh parsley

$1/2$ cup chopped fresh coriander

$1/2$ pound spaghetti

8 teaspoons freshly squeezed lemon juice, for garnish

PREPARATION

1. Transfer the chickpeas to a colander and rinse with cold water.

2. In a large soup pot, heat the olive oil over low heat. Add the onion, garlic, celery, and $1/2$ teaspoon salt and cook until soft.

3. Add the beef, marrow, chickpeas, and lentils, and mix well. Mix in the tomatoes and tomato paste and cook for 3 minutes.

4. Pour in the water and bring to a boil over high heat. Reduce heat, cover, and simmer for 2 hours.

5. Place the flour in a bowl and pour in 2 cups warm soup. Mix well, until all the flour dissolves and the mixture is lump-free. Pour flour-soup mixture back into the pot and stir.

6. Mix in the parsley, coriander, salt, and pepper. Break the spaghetti with your hands and add to the soup. Cook uncovered on low heat for 20 minutes.

7. Add salt and pepper to taste and transfer to serving bowls. Pour lemon juice over each serving and serve immediately.

FENNEL AND CHICKPEA SOUP

Cooked fennel has a delicate flavor and lovely texture. Garnish with grated Parmesan cheese or drizzle olive oil over top before serving.

INGREDIENTS

Serves 6

2 cups dried chickpeas, soaked overnight in 8 cups cold water

2 tablespoons extra virgin olive oil

1 onion, chopped

2 cloves garlic, minced

2 celery stalks, chopped

Salt and freshly ground black pepper

4 medium fennel bulbs, cut into 1/4-inch strips

$\frac{1}{2}$ cup white wine

$2\frac{1}{2}$ cups cold water

2 tablespoons chicken soup powder

PREPARATION

1. Transfer the chickpeas to a colander and rinse with cold water.

2. In a large soup pot, heat the olive oil over low heat, Add the onion, garlic, celery, and $\frac{1}{2}$ teaspoon salt and cook until soft. Mix in the fennel and cook until soft.

3. Pour in the wine, increase the heat, and cook for 5 minutes, or until the liquid evaporates.

4. Add the chickpeas and water, and bring to a boil.

5. Reduce heat, add soup powder, salt, and pepper. Cover and simmer for 2 hours.

6. Transfer to serving bowls and garnish with pepper.

MINESTRONE WITH CHICKPEAS

This Italian classic is traditionally made from whatever vegetables are in season, so feel free to adapt. Perfect for preparing in advance, this soup stores well for up to 48 hours in the refrigerator.

INGREDIENTS

Serves 6

2 cups dried chickpeas, soaked overnight in 8 cups cold water

13 cups cold water

1 teaspoon baking powder

1 pound tomatoes

3 tablespoons extra virgin olive oil, plus extra for garnish

1 red onion, coarsely chopped

2 carrots, peeled and cubed

3 celery stalks, cubed

2 sweet red peppers, cubed

2 cloves garlic, crushed

Salt and freshly ground black pepper

$\frac{1}{2}$ pound shell pasta

2 tablespoons chicken soup powder

$\frac{1}{4}$ cup fresh parsley, chopped

8 fresh basil leaves, chopped

1 tablespoon grated Parmesan cheese

PREPARATION

1. Drain the chickpeas, rinse, and transfer to a large pot. Add 8 cups water and baking powder, and bring to a boil over high heat. Reduce heat to low and cook uncovered for $1\frac{1}{2}$ hours, or until the chickpeas are almost soft. Drain and set aside.

2. In the meantime, boil 3 cups water in a small pot. Plunge the tomatoes in the boiling water for about 30 seconds, then transfer to a bowl of ice water. When the tomatoes are cool enough to handle, pierce with a sharp knife and peel away the skin. Cut into coarse cubes.

3. In a large soup pot, heat the olive oil over medium heat. Add the onion, carrot, celery, red peppers, garlic, and $\frac{1}{2}$ teaspoon salt, and cook until soft and slightly golden.

4. Add the pasta, tomatoes, soup powder, remaining 2 cups water, and chickpeas, and bring to a boil over high heat. Reduce heat and cook for 40 minutes.

5. Add the parsley, basil, salt, and pepper. Transfer to serving bowls and garnish with Parmesan.

PEA AND CHICKPEA SOUP

Adding chickpeas to this traditional favorite gives it a distinct appearance and nutty flavor.

INGREDIENTS

Serves 6

1 cup dried chickpeas, soaked overnight in 5 cups cold water

1 cup dried peas, soaked overnight in 5 cups cold water

2 tablespoons extra virgin olive oil, plus extra for garnish

1 onion, chopped

2 cloves garlic, minced

2 celery stalks, chopped

Salt and freshly ground white pepper

2½ cups cold water

2 tablespoons chicken soup powder

1 tablespoon chopped fresh parsley, plus extra olive oil for garnish

PREPARATION

1. Transfer the chickpeas and peas to a colander and rinse with cold water.

2. In a large soup pot, heat the olive oil over low heat. Add the onion, garlic, celery, and ½ teaspoon salt and cook until soft.

3. Add the chickpeas, peas, and water, and bring to a boil over high heat.

4. Reduce heat, add soup powder, salt, and pepper. Cover and simmer for 2 hours.

5. Transfer to serving bowls and garnish with fresh parsley and olive oil.

68

SPINACH AND CHICKPEA SOUP

Topped with a cube of fresh butter, this soup is creamy and comforting.

INGREDIENTS

Serves 6

2 cups dried chickpeas, soaked overnight in 8 cups cold water

2 tablespoons extra virgin olive oil

1 onion, chopped

2 cloves garlic, minced

Salt and freshly ground white pepper

½ pound fresh spinach leaves

2½ cups cold water

3 large potatoes, peeled and cut into ½-inch dice

1 tablespoon sweet paprika

2 tablespoons chicken soup powder

6 ½-inch dice of butter, for garnish

PREPARATION

1. Transfer the chickpeas to a colander, rinse with cold water, and set aside.

2. In a large soup pot, heat the olive oil over low heat. Add the onion, garlic, and ½ teaspoon salt, and cook until soft. Add the chickpeas and spinach and mix well.

3. Add the water, potatoes, paprika, salt, and pepper, and bring to a boil over high heat.

4. Reduce heat and add the soup powder. Cover and simmer for 2 hours.

5. Transfer to serving bowls and garnish each serving with a cube of butter.

FRESH HERB AND CHICKPEA SOUP

With a medley of fresh garden herbs, this soup is aromatic, light, and flavorful.
Serve with fresh whole-wheat bread or crispy crostini (page 13).

INGREDIENTS

Serves 6

2 cups dried chickpeas, soaked overnight in 8 cups cold water

2 tablespoons extra virgin olive oil, plus extra for garnish

1 onion, chopped

1 clove garlic, minced

2 celery stalks, chopped

Salt and freshly ground black pepper

2 tablespoons chopped fresh parsley

2 tablespoons chopped fresh basil leaves

1 tablespoon chopped fresh thyme leaves

$\frac{1}{2}$ tablespoon chopped fresh oregano leaves

$2\frac{1}{2}$ cups cold water

2 tablespoons chicken soup powder

2 tablespoons grated Parmesan cheese, for garnish

PREPARATION

1. Transfer the chickpeas to a colander and rinse with cold water.

2. In a large soup pot, heat the olive oil over low heat. Add the onion, garlic, celery, and $\frac{1}{2}$ teaspoon salt, and cook until soft. Add the parsley, basil, thyme, and oregano and mix well.

3. Add the chickpeas and water, and bring to a boil over high heat.

4. Reduce the heat and add soup powder, salt, and pepper. Cover and simmer for 2 hours.

5. Transfer to serving bowls, and garnish with olive oil, pepper, and Parmesan.

PUMPKIN AND CHICKPEA SOUP

This soup is perfect for serving on a brisk autumn day, when bright orange pumpkins and crisp green apples are in season.

INGREDIENTS

Serves 6

2 tablespoons extra virgin olive oil, plus extra for garnish

2 pounds fresh pumpkin or butternut squash, peeled, seeded, and cut into large chunks

4 large Granny Smith apples, peeled, seeded, and cut into large cubes

1 onion, chopped

3 tablespoons chicken soup powder

1 tablespoon soy sauce

1 tablespoon Worcestershire sauce

Pinch hot paprika

Salt and freshly ground black pepper

1 16-ounce can chickpeas, drained

Chopped coriander, for garnish

6 ½-inch dice of butter, for garnish

PREPARATION

1. In a large soup pot, heat the olive oil over low heat. Add the pumpkin, apples, and onion, and cook until they begin to soften.

2. Add enough water to cover the vegetables. Add the soup powder, soy sauce, Worcestershire sauce, paprika, 1 teaspoon salt, and a pinch of pepper, and bring to a boil.

3. Reduce heat and cook until the vegetables are completely soft.

4. Remove from the heat and purée with an immersion blender until smooth.

5. Warm the chickpeas by placing them in boiling water for 2 or 3 minutes. Drain and mix into the soup using a wooden spoon.

6. Transfer to soup bowls, garnish each serving with coriander and a cube of butter, and serve warm.

ENTRÉES

LAMB STEW WITH CHICKPEAS, RICE, AND WHEAT

This recipe is perfect for preparing in advance, as the flavors taste even better after they've had a chance to blend overnight. Transfer to a clean container with a tight-fitting lid before refrigerating.

INGREDIENTS

Serves 6

2 cups dried chickpeas, soaked overnight in 8 cups cold water

8 cups cold water

1 teaspoon baking powder

3 tablespoons extra virgin olive oil

1 onion, coarsely chopped

2 celery stalks, chopped

2 carrots, peeled and chopped

2 cloves garlic, crushed

Salt and freshly ground black pepper

1 pound lamb shoulder, cut into large chunks

$\frac{1}{2}$ cup rice

$\frac{1}{2}$ cup wheat berries

1 cup white wine

2 tablespoons tomato paste

1 tablespoon chicken soup powder

$\frac{1}{4}$ cup fresh chopped parsley

PREPARATION

1. Drain the chickpeas, rinse, and transfer to a large pot. Add the water and baking powder, and bring to a boil over high heat. Reduce heat to low and cook uncovered for $1\frac{1}{2}$ hours, or until the chickpeas are almost soft. Remove from the heat, drain, and set aside.

2. Preheat the oven to 400°F.

3. Heat the olive oil over low heat in a large ovenproof pan. Add the onion, celery, carrots, garlic, 1 teaspoon salt, and cook until soft. Add the lamb, rice, wheat berries, and chickpeas, and mix well.

4. Pour in the wine and increase heat. Cook until the liquid reduces by about half.

5. Add the tomato paste, soup powder, salt, and pepper, and bring to a boil over high heat.

6. Remove from the heat, cover, and transfer to the oven. Bake for $1\frac{1}{2}$ hours, or until the lamb is very soft.

7. Carefully remove from the oven and add parsley, salt, and pepper. Set aside to cool for 30 minutes.

8. Using a wide kitchen spoon, transfer a spoonful of rice and chickpeas to a dish. Top with lamb and serve warm.

BAKED CHICKEN AND CHICKPEAS

This is a great twist on traditional oven-baked chicken. Serve with a side of steamed rice or roasted potatoes.

INGREDIENTS

Serves 4

1 cup dried chickpeas, soaked overnight in 5 cups cold water

7 cups cold water

1 teaspoon baking powder

3 tablespoons extra virgin olive oil

1 onion, coarsely chopped

2 carrots, peeled and cut into $\frac{1}{4}$-inch dice

1 small celery heart, cut into $\frac{1}{4}$-inch dice

2 cloves garlic, crushed

1 fresh whole chicken

Salt and freshly ground black pepper

1 teaspoon ground cumin

1 cup white wine

PREPARATION

1. Drain the chickpeas, rinse, and transfer to a large pot. Add 5 cups water and baking powder, and bring to a boil over high heat. Reduce heat to low and cook uncovered for $1\frac{1}{2}$ hours, or until the chickpeas are almost soft. Remove from the heat, drain, and set aside.

2. Preheat the oven to 400°F.

3. Heat the olive oil over low heat in a large ovenproof pot. Add the onion, carrots, celery, and garlic, and cook until soft.

4. Place the chicken in the pot and season with 1 teaspoon salt, $\frac{1}{2}$ teaspoon pepper, and cumin.

5. Pour in the wine, increase heat, and cook for 3 minutes, or until the alcohol evaporates.

6. Use some of the chickpeas to stuff the chicken and pour the rest over top. Pour in remaining 2 cups water and bring to a boil over high heat. Cover the pot and transfer to the oven for 1 hour.

7. Transfer to a large dish and serve immediately.

CURRIED CHICKPEAS

This dish calls for Thai fish sauce, known as **nam bplah** *in Thai. It is an aromatic, salty, and distinct sauce that can be found in many large supermarkets and Asian food stores.*

INGREDIENTS

Serves 6

2 cups dried chickpeas, soaked overnight in 8 cups cold water

8½ cups cold water

1 teaspoon baking powder

2 tablespoons canola oil

1 onion, finely chopped

1 red pepper, cut into ¼-inch dice

2 cloves garlic, minced

3 tablespoons red curry paste

1 teaspoon sesame oil

1 tablespoon chopped fresh lemongrass

1 tablespoon chopped fresh coriander

½ teaspoon salt

1 teaspoon soy sauce

1 tablespoon Thai fish sauce

4 tablespoons fresh lime juice

PREPARATION

1. Drain the chickpeas, rinse, and transfer to a large pot. Add 8 cups water and baking powder, and bring to a boil over high heat. Reduce heat to low and cook uncovered for 1½ hours, or until the chickpeas are almost soft. Remove from the heat, drain, and set aside.

2. Heat the canola oil in a large pot and lightly sauté the onion and pepper until soft. Mix in the garlic, curry paste, and sesame oil, and cook for 3 minutes.

3. Add the lemongrass, coriander, chickpeas, and remaining ½ cup water, and bring to a boil over high heat.

4. Add the salt, soy sauce, fish sauce, and lime juice, and cook over low heat for 20 minutes.

5. Check taste and texture at this point. The curry should be thick, not runny. If necessary, cook for another 10 minutes over low heat.

6. Serve warm and be sure to warn guests that this dish is hot!

SPAGHETTI WITH FENNEL AND CHICKPEAS

Fennel is prized in Mediterranean cuisine for its delicate flavor and distinct texture. Although often compared with anise, fennel comes from a totally different plant, and is more closely related to parsley.

INGREDIENTS

Serves 6

1 cup dried chickpeas, soaked overnight in 5 cups cold water

8 cups cold water

1 teaspoon baking powder

4 tablespoons extra virgin olive oil

4 cloves garlic, minced

4 fennel bulbs, cut into $\frac{1}{2}$-inch slices

1 teaspoon salt

$\frac{1}{2}$ teaspoon freshly ground pepper

1 cup white wine

12 fresh basil leaves, coarsely chopped

2 tablespoons chopped fresh parsley

1 tablespoon coarse salt

1 pound spaghetti

$\frac{1}{4}$ cup grated Parmesan cheese

PREPARATION

1. Drain the chickpeas, rinse, and transfer to a large pot. Add 5 cups water and baking powder, and bring to a boil over high heat. Reduce heat to low and cook uncovered for $1\frac{1}{2}$ hours, or until the chickpeas are almost soft. Remove from the heat, drain, and set aside.

2. Heat the olive oil in a large pot over medium heat. Add the garlic and cook for 3 minutes.

3. Add the fennel, salt, and pepper, and cook for 10 minutes.

4. Pour in the wine and cook for 15 minutes.

5. Add the chickpeas, basil, and parsley, and cook over low heat for 30 minutes.

6. Separately, place the remaining 3 cups water and coarse salt in a large pot and bring to a boil. Add the spaghetti and cook according to the instructions on the package.

7. Drain the spaghetti and transfer to the pot with the sauce. Add the Parmesan and mix well. Transfer to individual serving dishes and serve immediately.

SHELL PASTA IN CHICKPEA AND TOMATO SAUCE

Add chickpeas to any pasta sauce to increase its nutritional value and enhance its texture. In this dish, the chickpeas are almost hidden by the shell pasta, but their distinct flavor is impossible to miss.

INGREDIENTS

Serves 6

1 cup dried chickpeas, soaked overnight in 5 cups cold water

8 cups cold water

1 teaspoon baking powder

4 tablespoons extra virgin olive oil

4 cloves garlic, minced

1 16-ounce can plum tomatoes, peeled and diced

1 teaspoon salt

$\frac{1}{2}$ teaspoon freshly ground black pepper

12 fresh basil leaves, coarsely chopped

1 tablespoon coarse salt

1 pound shell pasta

$\frac{1}{4}$ cup grated Parmesan cheese

PREPARATION

1. Drain the chickpeas, rinse, and transfer to a large pot. Add 5 cups water and baking powder, and bring to a boil over high heat. Reduce heat to low and cook uncovered for $1\frac{1}{2}$ hours, or until the chickpeas are almost soft. Remove from the heat, drain, and set aside.

2. Heat the olive oil in a large pot over medium heat. Add the garlic and cook for 3 minutes. Add the tomatoes, salt, and pepper, and cook for 10 minutes.

3. Add the chickpeas and basil and cook over low heat for 30 minutes.

4. Separately, place the remaining 3 cups water and coarse salt in a large pot and bring to a boil. Add the pasta and cook according to the instructions on the package.

5. Drain the pasta and transfer to the pot with the sauce. Transfer to individual serving dishes, top with Parmesan, and serve immediately.

BEEF AND CHICKPEA CASSEROLE

This dish bakes for about 1 1/2 hours, just the right amount of time for the beef shoulder to become perfectly tender and juicy.

INGREDIENTS

Serves 6

2 cups dried chickpeas, soaked overnight in 8 cups cold water

8 cups cold water

1 teaspoon baking powder

$\frac{1}{4}$ cup all-purpose flour

Salt and freshly ground black pepper

2 pounds beef shoulder, cut into 1-inch diced

$\frac{1}{4}$ cup canola oil

1 onion, finely chopped

2 celery stalks, diced

3 carrots, peeled and diced

2 cloves garlic, crushed

2 cups red wine

2 tablespoons tomato paste

2 tablespoons chicken soup powder

3 tablespoons extra virgin olive oil

$\frac{1}{4}$ cup chopped fresh parsley

PREPARATION

1. Drain the chickpeas, rinse, and transfer to a large pot. Add the water and baking powder, and bring to a boil over high heat. Reduce heat to low and cook uncovered for $1\frac{1}{2}$ hours, or until the chickpeas are almost soft. Drain and set aside.

2. Preheat the oven to 400°F.

3. Combine flour with salt and pepper in a shallow bowl. Roll the beef cubes in the flour mixture until completely coated.

4. Heat the canola oil in a large ovenproof pan until hot enough for frying. You'll know the oil is ready when the beef sizzles on contact. Brown the beef on all sides until golden, sealing in the juices. Remove using a slotted spoon and set aside.

5. Discard the oil and return the pan to the heat. Do not clean the pan. Add the onion, celery, carrots, garlic, and salt, and cook over low heat until soft.

6. Pour in the wine and increase heat. Cook until the liquid reduces by about half.

7. Add the beef, tomato paste, soup powder, chickpeas, olive oil, parsley, 1 teaspoon salt, and $\frac{1}{2}$ teaspoon pepper, and bring to a boil over high heat.

8. Remove the pan from the heat, cover, and transfer to the oven. Bake for $1\frac{1}{2}$ hours.

9. Add salt and pepper to taste, transfer to a deep serving dish, and serve immediately.

MEATBALLS IN SPICY CHICKPEA SAUCE

Serve this spicy variation of the traditional favorite with spaghetti, macaroni, or mashed potatoes.

INGREDIENTS

Serves 6

2 cups dried chickpeas, soaked overnight in 8 cups cold water

8 cups cold water

1 teaspoon baking powder

1 pound fresh beef, coarsely ground

1 large egg

$\frac{1}{4}$ cup bread crumbs

Salt and freshly ground black pepper

1 teaspoon sweet paprika

1 teaspoon cumin

1 16-ounce can whole plum tomatoes, peeled

3 tablespoons extra virgin olive oil

1 onion, coarsely chopped

2 celery stalks, finely chopped

2 cloves garlic, chopped

$\frac{1}{2}$ cup red wine

1 chili pepper, chopped

$\frac{1}{4}$ cup chopped fresh parsley

PREPARATION

1. Drain the chickpeas, rinse, and transfer to a large pot. Add water and baking powder, and bring to a boil over high heat. Reduce heat to low and cook uncovered for $1\frac{1}{2}$ hours, or until the chickpeas are soft. Remove from the heat and drain.

2. Transfer the chickpeas to the bowl of a food processor fitted with the steel blade and process until lightly crushed.

3. Transfer the chickpeas to a large bowl. Add the beef, egg, bread crumbs, 1 teaspoon salt, $\frac{1}{2}$ teaspoon pepper, paprika, and cumin. Mix well with your hands until uniform.

4. Wet your hands and roll the beef mixture into 1-inch balls. Arrange the balls on a plate, cover with plastic wrap, and refrigerate until ready to use.

5. Place the tomatoes in the bowl of a food processor fitted with the steel blade and process until crushed.

6. Separately, heat the olive oil over medium heat in a large pan. Add the onion, celery, and garlic, and cook until soft.

7. Add the tomatoes, wine, and 1 teaspoon salt, and cook over high heat for 3 minutes. Mix in the chili pepper and bring to a boil.

8. Reduce heat to low and carefully add the meatballs to the sauce. Cook for 1 hour.

9. Add the parsley and mix well. Add salt and pepper to taste and cook for 5 minutes. Transfer to a deep dish and serve immediately.

SPANISH RICE WITH CHICKPEAS

Deceptively simple to prepare, this dish makes a great impression and leaves a lovely aroma in your kitchen.

INGREDIENTS

Serves 6

2 cups dried chickpeas, soaked overnight in 8 cups cold water

11 cups cold water

1 teaspoon baking powder

$\frac{1}{3}$ cup extra virgin olive oil

2 cups long-grain rice

2 ripe tomatoes, finely diced

1 tablespoon salt

1 teaspoon freshly ground black pepper

1 tablespoon sweet paprika

2 tablespoons chicken soup powder

2 heads garlic

PREPARATION

1. Drain the chickpeas, rinse, and transfer to a large pot. Add 8 cups water and baking powder, and bring to a boil over high heat. Reduce heat to low and cook uncovered for $1\frac{1}{2}$ hours, or until the chickpeas are almost soft. Remove from the heat, drain, and set aside.

2. Preheat the oven to 400°F.

3. Heat the olive oil over medium heat in a 14-inch ovenproof pot with a tight-fitting lid for 3 minutes.

4. Stir in the rice and cook while stirring for 3 minutes.

5. Mix in the tomatoes, salt, and pepper, and cook for 3 minutes.

6. Add the paprika, chickpeas, soup powder, and remaining 3 cups water, and mix well.

7. Place the heads of garlic in the middle of the pot. Cover and transfer to the oven for 16 minutes.

8. Add salt and pepper to taste and serve warm.

OSSO BUCCO AND CHICKPEAS

The name of this classic Italian dish literally means "bone with a hole", or "hollow bones". Perfect for preparing in advance, it becomes even more tender and flavorful after the flavors have had a chance to sit overnight.

INGREDIENTS

Serves 6

2 cups dried chickpeas, soaked overnight in 8 cups cold water

10 cups cold water

1 teaspoon baking powder

1/4 cup all-purpose flour

Salt and freshly ground black pepper

6 slices veal shank, with bone

1/4 cup canola oil

1 red onion, sliced into rings

3 celery stalks, diced

2 carrots, peeled and diced

2 cloves garlic, crushed

2 cups white wine

1 16-ounce can coarsely chopped tomatoes

2 tablespoons chicken soup powder

3 tablespoons extra virgin olive oil

1/4 cup chopped fresh parsley

1 tablespoon chopped fresh thyme leaves

PREPARATION

1. Drain the chickpeas, rinse, and transfer to a large pot. Add 8 cups water and baking powder, and bring to a boil over high heat. Reduce heat to low and cook uncovered for 1 1/2 hours, or until the chickpeas are almost soft. Remove from the heat, drain, and set aside.

2. Preheat the oven to 400°F.

3. Combine flour with salt and pepper in a shallow bowl. Press each slice of veal into the flour mixture to coat.

4. Heat the canola oil over medium heat in a heavy, flat-bottom ovenproof pot. You'll know the oil is ready when the veal sizzles on contact. Brown the veal on both sides to seal in the juices. Remove using a slotted spoon and set aside. Discard the oil and return the pot to the heat. Do not clean the pot.

5. Add the onion, celery, carrots, garlic, and salt and cook over low heat until soft.

6. Pour in the wine and increase heat. Cook until the liquid reduces by about half.

7. Return the veal to the pot, arranging the pieces so that they do not overlap.

8. Add the tomatoes, remaining 2 cups water, soup powder, olive oil, parsley, thyme, salt, and pepper, and bring to a boil over high heat.

9. Transfer to the oven and bake covered for 1 1/2 hours, or until the veal is very soft. Increase heat to 450°F and bake uncovered for 15 minutes, or until the veal is a tempting golden color.

10. To serve, transfer a single veal shank to each serving plate. Accompany with a large scoop of chickpeas and pour sauce generously over both.

COD FILLET AND CHICKPEAS

With its low fat content and high level of omega-3 fatty acids, cod is an excellent choice for people interested in good health and great taste.

INGREDIENTS

Serves 6

2 cups dried chickpeas, soaked overnight in 8 cups cold water

8 cups cold water

1 teaspoon baking powder

3 tablespoons extra virgin olive oil, plus more for garnish

1 onion, coarsely chopped

2 celery stalks with leaves, cut into 1/4-inch dice

2 cloves garlic, crushed

2 pounds fresh cod fillet, cut into 2-inch dice

1 cup white wine

Salt and freshly ground black pepper

1/4 cup chopped fresh parsley

3 tablespoons freshly squeezed lemon juice

PREPARATION

1. Drain the chickpeas, rinse, and transfer to a large pot. Add the water and baking powder, and bring to a boil over high heat. Reduce heat to low and cook uncovered for 1 1/2 hours, or until the chickpeas are almost soft. Remove from the heat, drain, and set aside.

2. Heat the olive oil over medium heat in a large pan. Add the onion, celery, and garlic, and cook until soft.

3. Add the chickpeas, cod, wine, salt, and pepper, and cook over low heat for 20 minutes.

4. Mix in the parsley and lemon juice, and cook for 5 minutes. Transfer to a deep dish, drizzle with olive oil, and serve immediately.

BEEF TENDERLOIN WITH CHICKPEAS AND VEGETABLES

*The addition of chickpeas and lentils brings a Mediterranean flavor to the
traditional steak supper.*

INGREDIENTS

Serves 6

1 cup dried chickpeas, soaked overnight in 5 cups cold water

6 cups cold water

1 teaspoon baking powder

3 tablespoons extra virgin olive oil

1 onion, coarsely chopped

1 carrot, peeled and finely chopped

2 celery stalks with leaves, finely chopped

1 small celery heart, cut into $\frac{1}{4}$-inch dice

2 cloves garlic, crushed

$\frac{1}{2}$ cup dried green lentils, picked over and rinsed

1 cup red wine

Salt and freshly ground black pepper

1 ripe tomato, cut into $\frac{1}{2}$-inch dice

1 tablespoon tomato paste

6 4-ounce slices beef tenderloin

$\frac{1}{2}$ teaspoon coarse salt

2 scallions, green parts only, thinly sliced lengthwise, for garnish

PREPARATION

1. Drain the chickpeas, rinse, and transfer to a large pot. Add 5 cups water and baking powder, and bring to a boil over high heat. Reduce heat to low and cook uncovered for 1 hour, or until the chickpeas are almost soft. Remove from the heat, drain, and set aside.

2. Preheat the oven to 450°F.

3. Heat the olive oil in a large pan over medium heat. Add the onion, carrot, celery, celery heart, and garlic, and cook until soft.

4. Add the chickpeas, lentils, wine, 1 teaspoon salt, and $\frac{1}{2}$ teaspoon pepper, and cook over low heat for 10 minutes.

5. Pour in remaining cup water and bring to a boil over high heat. Add the tomato and tomato paste and cook for 40 minutes, or until most of the liquid has been absorbed and the chickpeas and lentils are soft. If necessary, add a little more liquid and cook for 10 more minutes. Add salt and pepper to taste.

6. Separately, heat a heavy skillet over high heat. Season the beef with coarse salt and pepper and brown on each side for about 3 minutes to seal in the juices.

7. Transfer the beef to a baking dish and bake for 10 minutes in a conventional oven, or 6 minutes in a convection oven.

8. Place a spoonful of the chickpea mixture on a plate and sprinkle with scallions. Top with the beef and serve immediately.

PORK CHOPS WITH CHICKPEAS AND CHARD

Enhance the elegance of everyday pork chops by combining them with fresh chard and nutty chickpeas.

INGREDIENTS

Serves 6

2 cups dried chickpeas, soaked overnight in 8 cups cold water

$8\frac{1}{2}$ cups cold water

1 teaspoon baking powder

3 tablespoons extra virgin olive oil

1 onion, coarsely chopped

2 cloves garlic, crushed

4 chard leaves, finely chopped

Salt and freshly ground black pepper

1 tablespoon soy sauce

2 tablespoons freshly squeezed lemon juice

Coarse salt

6 boneless pork chops

PREPARATION

1. Drain the chickpeas, rinse, and transfer to a large pot. Add 8 cups water and baking powder, and bring to a boil over high heat. Reduce heat to low and cook uncovered for $1\frac{1}{2}$ hours, or until the chickpeas are almost soft. Remove from the heat, drain, and set aside.

2. Preheat the oven to 450°F.

3. Heat the olive oil in a large pan over medium heat. Add the onion and garlic and cook until soft. Add the chard and cook over low heat for 10 minutes.

4. Mix in the chickpeas, remaining $\frac{1}{2}$ cup water, 1 tea-spoon salt, and $\frac{1}{2}$ teaspoon pepper, and cook over low heat for 10 minutes. Add the soy sauce, lemon juice, salt and pepper to taste, and mix well.

5. Separately, heat a heavy skillet over high heat. There is no need to add oil. Season the pork chops with $\frac{1}{2}$ teaspoon coarse salt and $\frac{1}{2}$ teaspoon pepper, and brown on each side for about 3 minutes to seal in the juices.

6. Transfer the pork chops to a baking dish and bake for 20 minutes in a conventional oven or 14 minutes in a convection oven.

7. To serve, place a heaping spoonful of the chickpea and chard mixture on a plate. Slice each pork chop, place over top, and serve immediately.

CHICKPEA CASSOULET

With lamb, bacon, and sausage, this dish is perfect for meat-lovers. It's also great for preparing in advance, as the flavors taste even better after they've had a chance to sit overnight.

INGREDIENTS

Serves 10

2 cups dried chickpeas, soaked overnight in 8 cups cold water

16 cups cold water

1 teaspoon baking powder

1/4 cup all-purpose flour

1 1/2 pounds leg of lamb, cut into 2-inch pieces

2 tablespoons extra virgin olive oil

1/2 pound salted bacon, cut into 1/2-inch dice

1 onion, coarsely chopped

2 carrots, peeled and cut into dice

2 celery stalks, cut into dice

2 cloves garlic, crushed

Salt and freshly ground black pepper

1 cup red wine

2 tablespoons tomato paste

2 tablespoons chicken soup powder

1 16-ounce can plum tomatoes, peeled and chopped

1 pound pure beef sausages

PREPARATION

1. Drain the chickpeas, rinse, and transfer to a large pot. Add 12 cups water and baking powder, and bring to a boil over high heat. Reduce heat to low and cook uncovered for 1 1/2 hours, or until the chickpeas are almost soft. Remove from the heat, drain, and set aside.

2. Preheat the oven to 400°F.

3. Place the flour in a shallow bowl and roll the lamb in the flour until coated.

4. Heat the olive oil in a large ovenproof pot over medium heat. You'll know the oil is ready when the lamb sizzles on contact. Cook the lamb until golden on all sides, then transfer to a large bowl and set aside.

5. Discard the oil and return the pot to the heat. Do not clean the pot. Add the bacon, onion, carrots, celery, garlic, salt, and pepper, and cook over low heat until soft.

6. Pour in the wine and increase heat to high. Cook for 3 minutes, or until the liquid reduces by about half.

7. Mix in the tomato paste and soup powder. Add the tomatoes and bring to a boil over high heat.

8. Add the chickpeas, remaining 4 cups water, and lamb. Cover and transfer to the oven for 1 hour.

9. In the meantime, heat a heavy skillet over medium heat. There is no need to add oil. Fry the sausages until golden and set aside.

10. Remove the lamb from the oven, top with the fried sausages, and return to the oven for 20 minutes. Add salt and pepper to taste and serve warm.

SNAPPER FILLET WITH CHICKPEAS AND LENTILS

Snapper is high in protein, vitamin B-12, and omega-3 fatty acids. Be sure not to overcook the snapper, so that the fish is moist and flavorful when served.

INGREDIENTS

Serves 6

1 cup dried chickpeas, soaked overnight in 8 cups cold water

8 cups cold water

1 teaspoon baking powder

4 tablespoons extra virgin olive oil

1 onion, coarsely chopped

1 carrot, peeled and finely chopped

2 celery stalks with leaves, finely chopped

2 cloves garlic, crushed

1 cup dried green lentils, picked over and rinsed

1 cup white wine

Salt and freshly ground white pepper

1 ripe tomato, cut into $\frac{1}{2}$-inch dice

6 5-ounce snapper fillets

3 tablespoons freshly squeezed lemon juice

PREPARATION

1. Drain the chickpeas, rinse, and transfer to a large pot. Add 5 cups water and baking powder, and bring to a boil over high heat. Reduce heat to low and cook uncovered for 1 hour, or until the chickpeas are almost soft. Remove from the heat, drain, and set aside.

2. Heat 3 tablespoons of olive oil over medium heat in a large pan. Add the onion, carrot, celery, and garlic, and cook until soft.

3. Add the chickpeas, lentils, wine, 1 teaspoon salt, and $\frac{1}{2}$ teaspoon pepper, and cook over low

heat for 10 minutes. Add remaining 3 cups water and bring to a boil over high heat.

4. Add the tomato and cook for 1 hour, or until most of the liquid has been absorbed and the chickpeas and lentils are soft. If necessary, add a little more liquid and cook for 10 more minutes. Add salt and pepper to taste.

5. In the meantime, preheat the oven to 400°F.

6. Brush the remaining tablespoon olive oil on a baking sheet and lay the snapper skin-side down. Season with salt and pepper and bake for 12 minutes, or until opaque.

7. Remove the snapper from the oven and pour lemon juice over top. Place a generous spoonful of the chickpea mixture on a plate, top with a piece of snapper, and serve immediately.

SALMON WITH SAFFRON AND CHICKPEAS

Saffron is the world's more treasured spice. Just a pinch of it in this recipe gives it a golden hue and distinct flavor.

INGREDIENTS

Serves 6

1 cup dried chickpeas, soaked overnight in 5 cups cold water

5 cups cold water

1 teaspoon baking powder

4 tablespoons extra virgin olive oil

2 cloves garlic, crushed

1 cup white wine

Pinch of saffron

Coarse salt and freshly ground white pepper

$1/2$ cup butter

6 6-ounce salmon fillets

1 tablespoon fresh rosemary leaves

2 tablespoons freshly squeezed lemon juice

PREPARATION

1. Drain the chickpeas, rinse, and transfer to a large pot. Add the water and baking powder, and bring to a boil over high heat. Reduce heat to low and cook uncovered for $1\frac{1}{2}$ hours, or until the chickpeas are almost soft. Remove from the heat, drain, and set aside.

2. Preheat the oven to 400°F.

3. Heat 3 tablespoons of olive oil in a large saucepan over low heat and lightly sauté the garlic for 3 minutes. Add the chickpeas, wine, saffron, 1 teaspoon coarse salt, and $1/2$ teaspoon pepper, and cook over low heat for 10 minutes. Add the butter and cook until melted.

4. Separately, brush the remaining tablespoon olive oil on a baking sheet. Season the salmon with salt and pepper and lay on the baking sheet. Sprinkle the rosemary over top and bake for 12 minutes.

5. Pour the lemon juice over the salmon just before serving. Place a spoonful of chickpeas on a plate, pour over a tablespoon of sauce, and top with a salmon fillet.

SEA BASS WITH CHICKPEAS AND FRESH HERBS

This recipe tastes best when made with fresh sea bass. Choose fillets with a salty sea scent and moist shiny scales.

INGREDIENTS

Serves 6

1 cup dried chickpeas, soaked overnight in 5 cups cold water

5 cups cold water

1 teaspoon baking powder

$\frac{1}{4}$ cup plus 2 tablespoons extra virgin olive oil

Coarse salt and freshly ground black pepper

2 cloves garlic

10 fresh basil leaves

1 tablespoon fresh oregano leaves

Handful fresh parsley

1 tablespoon fresh thyme leaves

6 sea bass fillets, with skin

2 tablespoons freshly squeezed lemon juice

Salt and freshly ground white pepper

PREPARATION

1. Drain the chickpeas, rinse, and transfer to a large pot. Add the water and baking powder, and bring to a boil over high heat. Reduce heat to low and cook uncovered for $1\frac{1}{2}$ hours, or until the chickpeas are soft. When the chickpeas are ready, remove from the heat. Drain, remove the peels of the chickpeas, and set aside.

2. Prepare the herb paste by placing $\frac{1}{2}$ cup olive oil, 1 teaspoon coarse salt, $\frac{1}{2}$ teaspoon black pepper, garlic, basil, oregano, parsley, and thyme in the bowl of a food processor or blender. Blend until smooth.

3. Remove 2 tablespoons of the herb paste and set aside. Pour the rest of the paste over the warm chickpeas, mix well, and set aside. It is important to pour the paste over the chickpeas while they are still warm, so that the flavors have a chance to blend.

4. Season the sea bass with salt and pepper. Heat a heavy pan with the remaining 2 tablespoons olive oil. When the oil is hot, place the sea bass skin-side down and sauté for 4 minutes on each side.

5. In the meantime, prepare the sauce by mixing the 2 tablespoons of paste set aside earlier with the lemon juice, 1 teaspoon salt, and $\frac{1}{2}$ teaspoon white pepper.

6. To serve, pile a generous spoonful of chickpeas on a serving plate. Top with a sea bass fillet and a tablespoon of sauce.

COUSCOUS WITH SEAFOOD AND CHICKPEAS

*The easiest way to make couscous is with a couscous pot or couscoussier. If you don't
have one, simply cook the meat and vegetables in a large pot with a tight-fitting lid.
Rest a colander inside the pot while the vegetables are cooking to steam the couscous.*

INGREDIENTS

Serves 6

1 cup dried chickpeas, soaked overnight in 5 cups cold water

8 cups cold water

1 teaspoon baking powder

4 tablespoons extra virgin olive oil

12 unshelled large shrimp

$\frac{1}{4}$ pound fresh calamari, bodies and tentacles

$\frac{1}{2}$ teaspoon coarse salt

2 onions, finely chopped

$\frac{1}{2}$ pound fresh black mussels, cleaned

Salt and freshly ground black pepper

2 tablespoons chopped fresh parsley

1 teaspoon chopped fresh oregano leaves

1 cup white wine

2 teaspoons sundried tomato paste

2 teaspoons chicken soup powder

2 cups instant couscous

1 red chili pepper, finely sliced

PREPARATION

1. Drain the chickpeas, rinse, and transfer to a large pot. Add 5 cups water and baking powder, and bring to a boil over high heat. Reduce heat to low and cook uncovered for $1\frac{1}{2}$ hours, or until the chickpeas are almost soft. Remove from the heat, drain, and set aside.

2. Heat 2 tablespoons of olive oil in a large heavy skillet over medium heat. Add the shrimp and calamari, sprinkle with the coarse salt, and sauté for 3 or 4 minutes on each side. Set aside.

3. Pour any remaining oil from the skillet into the bottom of a couscous pot. Add the onion and sauté over medium heat until translucent.

4. Add the mussels, 1 teaspoon salt, $\frac{1}{2}$ teaspoon pepper, 1 tablespoon parsley, oregano, wine, chickpeas, and sundried tomato paste, and mix well.

5. Add the remaining 3 cups water and soup powder and bring to a boil. Reduce heat to low and cook for 30 minutes.

6. Place the couscous in the top part of the couscous pot and steam for 10 minutes.

7. Remove the couscous and continue cooking the mussels and chickpeas for another 30 minutes.

8. Remove from the heat. Add the shrimp, calamari, couscous, remaining tablespoon parsley, and chili pepper, and mix well. Add salt and pepper to taste. Transfer to deep pasta dishes and serve immediately.

STUFFED CALAMARI

*Often coated and deep-fried when served in restaurants and cafés, calamari
tastes excellent when lightly sautéed. It also has far fewer calories and fat.*

INGREDIENTS

Serves 6

1 cup dried chickpeas, soaked overnight in 5 cups cold water

5 cups cold water

1 teaspoon baking powder

1 teaspoon finely chopped fresh thyme leaves

1 teaspoon finely chopped fresh oregano leaves

1 teaspoon finely chopped fresh basil leaves

Rind from 1 lemon, chopped

Salt and freshly ground black pepper

1 pound small whole calamari, cleaned and tentacles removed

3 ripe tomatoes

3 tablespoons extra virgin olive oil

1 onion, finely chopped

2 cloves garlic, minced

1 cup white wine

2 teaspoons sundried tomato paste

3 tablespoons freshly squeezed lemon juice

PREPARATION

1. Drain the chickpeas, rinse, and transfer to a large pot. Add the water and baking powder, and bring to a boil over high heat. Reduce heat to low and cook uncovered for $1\frac{1}{2}$ hours, or until the chickpeas are almost soft. Remove from the heat, drain, and set aside.

2. Place the chickpeas, thyme, oregano, basil, lemon rind, 1 teaspoon salt, and $\frac{1}{2}$ teaspoon pepper in a large bowl. Mix well using your hands until the chickpeas are evenly coated. Using your hands, stuff each calamari with the mixture and place on a large plate.

3. Preheat the oven to 375°F.

4. Place the tomatoes in the bowl of a food processor fitted with the steel blade. Grind coarsely and set aside.

5. Heat the olive oil in a large ovenproof pan over medium heat. Sauté the onion and garlic until soft.

6. Pour in the wine and cook over high heat 3 minutes. Add the tomatoes and tomato paste, and bring to a boil.

7. Remove pan from the heat and carefully place the stuffed calamari inside. Cover, transfer to the oven, and bake for 1 hour.

8. Add salt and pepper to taste and transfer to serving dishes. Garnish with fresh lemon juice and serve with a fresh salad of baby greens or arugula.

SPICY SCALLOPS AND CHICKPEAS

This dish calls for Thai fish sauce, known as **nam bplah** *in Thai. It is an aromatic, salty, and distinct sauce that can be found in many large supermarkets and Asian food stores.*

INGREDIENTS

Serves 6

2 cups dried chickpeas, soaked overnight in 8 cups cold water

8 cups cold water

1 teaspoon baking powder

2 tablespoons Thai fish sauce

1 teaspoon red curry paste

1 tablespoon sweet chili sauce

1 tablespoon sesame oil

1 green mango, peeled and cut into $\frac{1}{4}$-inch dice

1 tablespoon rice vinegar

1 tablespoon chopped fresh coriander

24 large scallops

$\frac{1}{2}$ teaspoon salt

$\frac{1}{2}$ teaspoon freshly ground black pepper

2 tablespoons freshly squeezed lime juice

PREPARATION

1. Drain the chickpeas, rinse, and transfer to a large pot. Add the water and baking powder, and bring to a boil over high heat. Reduce heat to low and cook uncovered for $1\frac{1}{2}$ hours, or until the chickpeas are almost soft. Remove from the heat and drain.

2. In a large deep pan, place the chickpeas, fish sauce, curry paste, chili sauce, and sesame oil. Sauté over high heat for 5 minutes while stirring.

3. Reduce the heat and add the mango, vinegar, and coriander. Mix well, remove from heat, and set aside.

4. Separately, heat a nonstick pan over high heat. There should be no oil in the pan. Season the scallops with salt and pepper and sauté for 3 minutes on each side. Remove from the heat and pour lime juice over the scallops.

5. To serve, place 2 tablespoons of the chickpea mixture in a deep pasta dish. Arrange four scallops over top and serve immediately.

PASTRIES AND OTHER SPECIALTIES

TRADITIONAL FALAFEL

Falafel is usually served in a pita with creamy tahini drizzled on top. To make perfectly round falafel balls, try using a falafel scoop, available in specialty cooking shops and Middle Eastern food stores.

INGREDIENTS

Serves 6

2 cups dried chickpeas, soaked overnight in 8 cups cold water

5 cloves garlic

1 tablespoon chopped fresh coriander

1 tablespoon chopped fresh parsley

1 teaspoon cumin

½ teaspoon baking powder

1 teaspoon salt

½ teaspoon freshly ground pepper

2 tablespoons breadcrumbs

1½ cups canola oil for frying

PREPARATION

1. Drain the chickpeas and place in the bowl of a food processor fitted with the steel blade.

2. Add the garlic, coriander, parsley, cumin, baking powder, salt, and pepper, and process until uniform.

3. Transfer to a large bowl, add the breadcrumbs, and mix well. Cover with plastic wrap and refrigerate for 30 minutes.

4. Pour the oil in an 8-inch pan and heat over medium heat. You'll know the oil is ready for frying when the mixture sizzles on contact.

5. With wet hands, form the chickpea mixture into 1-inch balls. Carefully place the balls in the hot oil and fry until golden brown. Transfer the falafel to a paper towel to remove excess oil, and serve warm.

FRESH HERB FALAFEL

These falafel have a bright green color and garden fresh flavor.

INGREDIENTS

Serves 6

2 cups dried chickpeas, soaked overnight in 8 cups cold water

5 cloves garlic

¼ cup chopped fresh coriander

¼ cup chopped fresh parsley

1 teaspoon fresh thyme leaves

1 teaspoon fresh oregano leaves

1 teaspoon cumin

½ teaspoon baking powder

1 teaspoon salt

½ teaspoon freshly ground pepper

2 tablespoons breadcrumbs

1½ cups canola oil for frying

PREPARATION

1. Drain the chickpeas and place in the bowl of a food processor fitted with the steel blade.

2. Add the garlic, coriander, parsley, thyme, oregano, cumin, baking powder, salt, and pepper, and process until uniform.

3. Transfer to a large bowl, add the breadcrumbs, and mix well. Cover with plastic wrap and refrigerate for 30 minutes.

4. Pour the oil in an 8-inch pan and heat over medium heat. You'll know the oil is ready when the mixture sizzles on contact.

5. Form the chickpea mixture into 1-inch balls using wet hands or a falafel scoop. Carefully place the balls in the hot oil and fry until golden brown. Transfer the falafel to a paper towel to remove excess oil, and serve warm.

FALAFEL WITH SUNDRIED TOMATOES

The addition of sundried tomato paste to this traditional favorite gives it a rusty color and distinct salty flavor.

INGREDIENTS

Serves 6

2 cups dried chickpeas, soaked overnight in 8 cups cold water

5 cloves garlic

1 tablespoon chopped fresh parsley

3 tablespoons sundried tomato paste

½ teaspoon baking powder

1 teaspoon salt

½ teaspoon freshly ground pepper

2 tablespoons breadcrumbs

1½ cups canola oil for frying

PREPARATION

1. Drain the chickpeas and place in the bowl of a food processor fitted with the steel blade.

2. Add the garlic, parsley, sundried tomato paste, baking powder, salt, and pepper, and process until uniform.

3. Transfer to a large bowl, add the breadcrumbs, and mix well. Cover with plastic wrap and refrigerate for 30 minutes.

4. Pour the oil in an 8-inch pan and heat over medium heat. You'll know the oil is ready when the mixture sizzles on contact.

5. Form the chickpea mixture into 1-inch balls using wet hands or a falafel scoop. Carefully place the balls in the hot oil and fry until golden brown. Transfer the falafel to a paper towel to remove excess oil, and serve warm.

MARSEILLE CHICKPEA BAKE

The chickpea flour in this recipe gives it a subtle nutty flavor. Cool before slicing and serve with fresh creamy butter.

INGREDIENTS

Serves 6

1¼ cups chickpea flour

1 cup cold water

1 teaspoon salt

2 tablespoons extra virgin olive oil

1 tablespoon canola oil

PREPARATION

1. Preheat the oven to 375°F.

2. Mix the flour, water, salt, and olive oil in a large bowl until uniform.

3. Brush the canola oil in a 10-inch round pan. Pour the batter evenly into the pan and transfer to the middle rack of your oven. Bake for 40 minutes in a conventional oven, or 25 minutes in a convection oven.

PANELLE

These deep-fried fritters are a traditional Sicilian treat. Serve warm with fresh yogurt or tangy tzatziki.

INGREDIENTS

Serves 6

3½ cups cold water

1 teaspoon salt

2 cups chickpea flour

1½ cups canola oil

PREPARATION

1. Place the water and salt in a large bowl and mix. Gradually add the flour, stirring constantly, until the batter is uniform and free of lumps. Refrigerate for 30 minutes.

2. Heat the oil over medium heat in a 10-inch pan. You'll know the oil is hot enough for frying when the batter sizzles on contact.

3. Fry 4 or 5 spoonfuls of the batter at a time, making sure they are each about 1 inch apart. Fry for about 4 minutes on each side, or until golden brown.

4. Transfer the panelle to a paper towel to remove excess oil, and serve warm.

CHICKPEAS IN PUFF PASTRY

*Buttery and flaky, these bacon, cheese, and spinach-stuffed snacks will be
finished moments after they come out of the oven. Look for all-butter puff pastry
in the freezer section of your supermarket.*

INGREDIENTS

Serves 6

1 tablespoon extra virgin
olive oil

1 pound fresh spinach leaves

½ pound smoked bacon, thinly
sliced and cut into ¼-inch
pieces

8 ounces canned chickpeas,
drained

2 large eggs

¼ cup grated Parmesan cheese

All-purpose flour, for dusting

1 pound puff pastry, frozen
and thawed

1 egg yolk

1 tablespoon water

PREPARATION

1. Preheat oven to 400°F.

2. Heat the olive oil in a heavy
skillet over medium heat. Add the
spinach and sauté for 3 minutes,
or until soft.

3. Transfer the spinach to a
colander and drain well, removing
as much liquid as possible.

4. Return the skillet to the heat
and fry the bacon over high heat
until golden.

5. In a large bowl, place the
spinach, chickpeas, bacon, eggs,
and Parmesan cheese and mix
well.

6. Lightly dust your work surface
with flour. Roll out half of the
puff pastry into a 10–by–5-inch
rectangle.

7. Spread half of the spinach
mixture along the 10-inch side of
the pastry and roll into a cylinder.
Roll the cylinder into a snail
shape. Repeat with the remaining
puff pastry and filling to make a
second pastry.

8. Mix together the egg yolk and
water and brush onto the pastries.
Place on a baking sheet and bake
for 30 minutes, or until golden
brown.

CHICKPEA PANCAKES

The use of chickpea flour in these pancakes makes them perfect for people who are gluten intolerant or looking for an alternative to white flour.

INGREDIENTS

Serves 6

3 large eggs

1 cup milk

1 tablespoon sugar

1 teaspoon salt

1 cup chickpea flour

2 tablespoons extra virgin olive oil

PREPARATION

1. In a large bowl, whisk together the eggs and milk. Add the sugar and salt and mix well.

2. Gradually add the flour, stirring constantly, until the batter is uniform and free of lumps. Pour in the olive oil and mix well.

3. Heat a nonstick pan over medium heat. There is no need to add oil. When the pan is hot, place several tablespoons of batter, making sure each is about 1 inch apart. Cook for 3 minutes on each side.

4. Serve pancakes warm, with sausages, cheese, or caviar.

FARINATA

*This flatbread is native to the Italian region of Liguria. It can be eaten plain
or topped with fresh rosemary, grated cheese, or sautéed onions.*

INGREDIENTS

Serves 10

2 1/2 cups chickpea flour

1 1/2 cups cold water

1/2 cup extra virgin olive oil

2 teaspoons salt

1 teaspoon freshly ground
white pepper

Rosemary or freshly ground
black pepper, for garnish

PREPARATION

1. Place the flour in a large bowl.
Gradually add the water while
stirring. Let rest for at least
4 hours.

2. Preheat the oven to 400°F.

3. A layer of foam will have
formed on the batter while it sat.
Remove the foam with a spoon
and mix well.

4. Brush the olive oil in a shallow
pan, making sure that the oil
covers the whole surface. Pour
the batter into the pan and mix
using a wooden spoon, so that
the oil is absorbed by the batter.
Sprinkle with salt and pepper and
bake until golden.

5. Garnish with rosemary or black
pepper. Cut into cubes and serve
immediately after baking.

CHICKPEA BREAD

There's nothing quite like the smell of baking bread to warm your house and whet your appetite. Serve with creamy butter or sweet jam.

INGREDIENTS

Serves 6

1 cup cold water

2 teaspoons dried yeast

1¼ cups chickpea flour

2 cups bread flour, plus more for dusting

2 teaspoons salt

1 tablespoon extra virgin olive oil

PREPARATION

1. Place the water, yeast, chickpea flour, and bread flour in the bowl of an electric mixer fitted with the dough hook. Knead on low speed for 3 minutes.

2. Add the salt and continue kneading on medium speed for 10 minutes.

3. Transfer the dough to a floured bowl, and cover with a kitchen towel. Set aside to rest in a warm place until it doubles in size, about 1 hour.

4. Turn the dough out onto a floured surface and punch it down to remove all the air. Roll the dough into a ball and place on a baking sheet lined with parchment paper. Cover with a kitchen towel, and let rest for 1 hour in a warm place.

5. Preheat the oven to 430°F.

6. Just before placing the bread in the oven, cut a crisscross pattern on the top using a serrated knife and dust lightly with flour. Bake for 30 minutes, or until golden brown. You'll know the bread is ready when it makes a hollow sound when tapped lightly on the bottom. Set aside to cool before slicing.

SAMBUSAK

This stuffed pastry is a traditional favorite all over the Middle East. Make smaller pockets for appetizers, or larger ones for a delicious side dish or snack.

INGREDIENTS

Serves 15

2 cups dried chickpeas, soaked overnight in 8 cups cold water

9 cups cold water

1 teaspoon baking powder

3 cups all-purpose flour, plus more for dusting

1 tablespoon dried yeast

1 tablespoon sugar

4 tablespoons extra virgin olive oil

$2\frac{1}{2}$ teaspoons salt

1 onion, finely diced

$\frac{1}{2}$ teaspoon black pepper

$\frac{1}{2}$ teaspoon cumin

2 tablespoons chopped fresh parsley

$1\frac{1}{2}$ cups canola oil for frying

PREPARATION

1. Drain the chickpeas, rinse, and transfer to a large pot. Add 8 cups water and baking powder, and bring to a boil over high heat. Reduce heat to low and cook uncovered for $1\frac{1}{2}$ hours, or until the chickpeas are almost soft. Remove from the heat, drain, and set aside.

2. To make the dough, place the flour, yeast, remaining cup water, sugar, and 2 tablespoons of olive oil in the bowl of an electric mixer. Using the dough hook, knead on low speed for 3 minutes.

3. Gradually add 2 teaspoons of salt while the mixer is operating. Increase speed to medium and knead for 8 minutes.

4. Transfer the dough to a floured bowl and cover with plastic wrap. Set aside for 45 minutes.

5. In the meantime, heat the remaining 2 tablespoons olive oil in a heavy skillet over medium heat. Add the onion and sauté until golden.

6. Add the chickpeas, $\frac{1}{2}$ teaspoon salt, pepper, and cumin, and mix well. Remove from heat, mix in the parsley, and set aside.

7. Turn the dough out onto a floured surface and press with the palm of your hand to remove all the air bubbles. Using a rolling pin, roll out the dough until it is about $\frac{1}{8}$ inch thick.

8. Cut out 3-inch circles from the dough using a glass or cutter. Knead together the scraps and cut out remaining circles.

9. Place a heaping tablespoon of the chickpea filling in the center of each circle. Fold the dough in half to make a pocket and pinch together the edges to seal.

10. Heat the canola oil in a pan over medium heat. You'll know the oil is ready for frying when the dough sizzles on contact. Fry each sambusak until golden and transfer to a paper towel to remove excess oil. Serve warm.

INDEX